ALWAYS ON

strategy+business

ALWAYS ON

Advertising, Marketing, and Media in an Era of Consumer Control

CHRISTOPHER VOLLMER
WITH GEOFFREY PRECOURT

New York   Chicago   San Francisco   Lisbon   London
Madrid   Mexico City   Milan   New Delhi   San Juan
Seoul   Singapore   Sydney   Toronto

1 2 3 4 5 6 7 8 9 0   DOC/DOC   0 9 8

ISBN 978-0-07-150828-5
MHID   0-07-150828-7

Design by Lee Fukui and Mauna Eichner

McGraw-Hill books are available at special quantity discounts to use as premiums and sales promotions, or for use in corporate training programs. To contact a representative please visit the Contact Us pages at www.mhprofessional.com.

To Jill, Ursula, and Mark

CONTENTS

THE TWENTY-FIRST-CENTURY MARKETING MIX

SINCE THE LATE 1980S, three little words and an iconic logo defined one of the world's most successful brands. The words were: "Just Do It." The logo was the famous Nike swoosh. Together they conveyed a competitive spirit and gritty brand image that gave consumers a memorable point of differentiation in a marketplace cluttered with seemingly similar products.

Nike and its advertising agency Wieden & Kennedy worked together to define and redefine that message, always staying one step ahead of the competition. But just as Nike evolved, so did its consumers. During the past few years, the game of marketing athletic shoes and apparel—and, for that matter, the game of marketing and advertising everything else—has changed profoundly.

"Gone are the days of 'one shoe, one advertising campaign.' Now you've got to engage consumers on every level," said Trevor Edwards, Nike's vice president of global brand and category management, in a 2007 interview with the *Wall Street Journal.* Gone, as well, is the exclusive one-on-one relationship between Nike and its sole advertising agency. Nike retained the agency as one of its anchor partners (W&K still supports Nike on key parts of the business such as basketball and football). But the company pulled its running shoe business out of W&K in March 2007 and awarded it instead to Crispin Porter & Bogusky. This Miami agency, a unit of MDC partners, won the account in part because of its reputation for applying creative skills to digital advertising.

As *Advertising Age* reported, "Neither Nike nor Wieden officials would get into specifics about the change, but a number of industry executives believe one area of concern for the marketer was Wieden's [lack of] interactive capabilities."

Over the last few years, Nike has been steadily increasing the role of digital media in its marketing mix. For example, in advance of the 2006 World Cup tournament, Nike teamed up with Google to launch an online social community targeting soccer fans and athletes. It was precisely the kind of interactive and viral media environment that spoke directly to the consumers with whom Nike most wanted to build relationships, with a precision and intimacy not available in television or print ads. Christened joga.com, the site recorded more than 110 million downloads of soccer-related information and media clips. The benefit for Nike? "We get right to the center of the consumer," Edwards observed.

Joga.com was just one of several innovative initiatives that transformed Nike's marketing and advertising prowess. Another was developed around Nike+, a joint venture between Nike and Apple that allows iPod users to monitor their workouts using a sensor in their Nike footwear, tracking their calorie-burning and heart rates in real time and online. In partnership with R/GA, a division of the Interpublic Group, Nike and Apple created nikeplus.com, an experiential, Web-based service that offers much more than just eye-catching advertising. On nikeplus.com, consumers could post their workout results, share favorite running routes, compare their efforts to those of professional athletes such as Lance Armstrong and LeBron James, and even download music mixed specifically to inspire and motivate. Nike+ effectively hit all of Nike's objectives: it was high on relevance; it was engineered for interactivity and community; and it was scalable, appealing to both serious runners and novices.

Nike's new marketing strategy is not just focused on online media. The company has invested about $2.5 billion in endorsement contracts extending through 2011, including sponsorships of golf master Tiger Woods, tennis champion Roger Federer, the Manchester United soccer team, and many other athletes and teams. The intent is to embed the Nike brand directly into sports content and to inoculate the "swoosh" against such threats as ad skipping. Nike is also actively experimenting with interactive TV. In the "Quick Is Deadly" campaign for its Zoom training shoe line, satellite-dish-based TV subscribers were offered exclusive programming of the San Diego Chargers' La Damian Tomlinson, a 3D demo of the Zoom shoe, and a Nike-branded interactive game designed to test their reflexes. Rounding out the package: a zip-code-driven search application to help consumers locate the closest store selling the Zoom. Finally, Nike is also upping its game through more "word-of-foot" marketing; it is sponsoring events such as the San Francisco marathon, soccer and basketball tournaments, and other amateur competitions where Nike marketers can connect directly with their target consumers, learn more about them, and create more brand advocates and loyalists.

In short, Nike's marketing playbook has moved from the flash of a brilliant tagline and a memorable logo to a focus on consumer experiences. And that approach is delivering results. From 2003 to 2006, Nike grew its U.S. revenues from about $4.6 billion to nearly $5.7 billion, or about 7 percent on an annualized basis. During that same period, its total U.S. advertising budget increased at about the same rate to $678 million. What mix of advertising drove this growth? A bigger emphasis on digital advertising, as well as investments in Nike's own Web sites, events, and other promotional efforts. In fact, the percentage of Nike's budget devoted to traditional media (such as TV and magazines) declined from 40 to 33 percent during those three years. The net effect: Nike's message is not just the advertising tacked on to consumer content. The advertising *is* the content.

"The Nike brand will always be our strongest asset, but consumers are looking for new relevance and connections," Mark Parker, Nike's CEO, told an audience of investors in March 2007. "It's really all about going deeper to get deeper connections and deeper insights, to get more innovation and more relevance, and to make us ultimately more competitive."

The active leadership of Nike's senior management in the development of a next-generation marketing strategy— including the CEO's willingness to attribute the competitiveness of the Nike brand to its more contemporary advertising playbook—has sent a strong message to the company's marketing and media partners. No matter how talented the creative team is, an agency relationship is suboptimal if it does not drive high-impact digital media into its advertising. Furthermore, digital must be a fundamental building block of the brand and advertising strategy; no longer can it be an add-on or an afterthought. And it also performs the vital function of keeping in closer touch with consumers, even if many of the old-style media and retail channels diminish or disappear in the process.

THE FUTURE IS NOW

Nike's shift in strategy is not happening in a vacuum. It's a calculated response to a set of driving forces in marketing and advertising, forces that have been building for years but were easy to ignore because they still hadn't quite hit. Now they have. We are now at the beginning of a consumer-centric digital age in which the traditional approaches to marketing products and services are no longer viable.

Consumers are in control; they have greater access to information and greater command over media consumption than ever before. The emergence of a host of new media— the Internet, DVRs, iPods, mobile phones, and other devices—has sharply constrained marketers' ability to use analog media (TV, radio, and print) to shape brand preferences and consumer behavior. The corporate demand for marketing accountability and return on investment has reached a crescendo. And the traditional relationships between marketers and their ad agencies are being redefined.

The emergence of new media, models, and metrics creates many challenges, but also opportunities for more effective marketing and advertising. For years, marketers have been waiting for practice to catch up with potential—for the arrival of technology and media formats that would enable better targeting, stronger accountability, and more granular consumer insight. Now the waiting is over, and the new operational reality will reshape every link in the media and marketing ecosystem.

Many companies recognize they need a new playbook and will, like Nike, make sweeping changes in the way they approach marketing, advertising, and consumers in general. The impact is already being felt in every consumer sector, from apparel to household goods to food to automobiles to appliances—and in business-to-business marketing as well. As business leaders see these changing trends affect their enterprises firsthand, they are fashioning new kinds of advertising and marketing for a new always-on era—anchored firmly in relevance, interactivity, and measurability.

As with the Internet that helped to shape it, the new environment is "always on" because the consumer is always present: constantly seeking opportunities and value, taking advantage of the multiplying media around it, and (at the same time) being bombarded with ever more media in ever more forms. Marketers are "always on" as well: they have no respite or downtime because the rapidly changing nature of their audiences—and the means of connecting with them—requires continual experimentation, innovation, and shifts in strategy.

Marketing in this era requires new strategies and tools to connect effectively with consumers. Instead of being satisfied with knowing how many people are exposed to their brand messages, some marketers are working hard to determine how well their messages are received, whether they're powerful enough to generate a customer response, and exactly what those responses are. They have learned a primary lesson of the always-on media environment: it doesn't matter how many people are watching; what counts is whether they're paying attention and responding. With knowledge of this kind, marketing is being reborn as a consumer-centered craft.

Finally, these marketers are shaking up the established order in their quest to capture the future. They are abandoning old partners in the media and in advertising whenever those partners cannot live up to the new imperatives of marketing's future.

The resulting renaissance is already taking place at a number of leading companies. Innovators in marketing, advertising, and media feel a profound sense of urgency to reinvent their professions *now*—through new skills, new positionings, and new relationships. You need only look at the dramatic steps companies such as Nike are taking to realize that the future of advertising and marketing is not coming—it is here.

Many others, however, still have a long way to go. For all the hype around digital advertising and media, for instance, the top 100 national advertisers in the United States allocate just 5 percent of their total measured media spending to online.

What's holding back the laggards? Many still have difficulty seeing beyond television. Marketing metrics and agency economics are still built around TV. TV is still the easiest way to get retail and trade partners excited. And many creative advertising people still think a 30-second

ALWAYS ON . . . EVERYWHERE

The Daniel Yankelovich Group estimates that an average citizen who lives in a city may encounter up to 5,000 advertising messages a day (see Exhibit 1-1). That translates to more than three each minute. It's a significant increase from the estimated 2,000 ads the same person would have seen during a day in the mid-1970s, when advertising focused on network TV, magazines, newspapers, and radio.

In 2007, the *New York Times* observed: "Supermarket eggs have been stamped with the names of CBS television shows. Subway turnstiles bear messages from Geico auto insurance. Chinese food cartons promote Continental Airways. US Airways is selling ads on motion sickness bags. And the trays used in airport security lines have been [promoting] Rolodexes . . . Consumers' viewing and reading habits are so scattershot now that many advertisers say the best way to reach time-pressed consumers is to try to catch their eye at literally every turn."

EXHIBIT 1-1 **THE EVERYWHERE PRESENCE OF ADVERTISING**

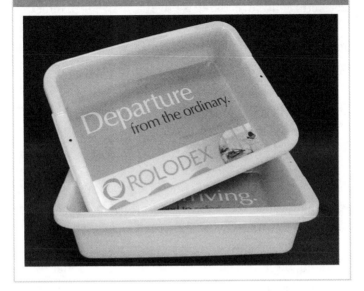

minimovie is the most powerful way to communicate with consumers.

There are other barriers that are more structural and internal to corporations. Metrics still are not comparable across media. Even in digital media, where metrics are a compelling part of the value proposition, they are rarely standardized and not well understood. By and large, marketers still lack the number-crunching skills needed to determine ROI. And too many companies still think of new media as an "experiment" rather than as a core component of brand-building and sales.

Viable responses to all these challenges are rapidly emerging. There is no commonly accepted single set of new practices to replace them, no silver bullet that can address

the challenge of brand building in the "always-on" digital era. But make no mistake: participation in the future of marketing and advertising is not optional; it is mandatory.

THE SUPER CMO

Even though nearly every marketer has a different take on the best way to make use of the new media, models, and metrics, there does seem to be across-the-board agreement on the starting point: the shape of the future of advertising and marketing is too novel, too important, and too dynamic to be left either to traditional marketing practices or to the long-established customs of media companies and ad agencies.

Who, then, will guide the future? One promising answer has been the emergence of a new class of highly capable chief marketing officers who are taking an active hand in building marketing models that are more ROI-focused, multiplatform, and targeted than ever before.

The "Super CMO," a term coined by Harvard Business School professors John Quelch and Gail McGovern in 2004, is a powerful new breed of marketer with a chair at the table of a company's senior management. These individuals are more media savvy and more focused on accountability than their predecessors; they insist on driving business performance, innovation, and results, not just advising or managing marketing campaigns and overseeing their advertising vendors. Because of their enhanced role, they are driving many of the changes occurring across the media and marketing ecosystem. These are the executives who are making demands—and expecting results—

from their media partners, their ad agencies, and their own brand teams. They're saying, "I need an integrated campaign. I need something that's a lot more compelling than a 30-second spot. I need something that delivers results." Absent the pressure of their insistence, the future might have taken much longer to arrive.

Perhaps the greatest change driver created by these Super CMOs is the high degree of accountability that they demand. This, in turn, has ended the paradoxical ambiguity of marketing during the twentieth century.

Beyond promotion ad spending, which is basically an experiment in retail pricing, it has always been difficult to know whether or how advertising moves brands and businesses. "Does advertising increase demand for a given firm's products?" asked Harvard Business School professor Neil Borden in his classic 1942 text, *The Economic Effects of Advertising*. "Indeterminate," he concluded. Does it preclude price competition? "In no case," he wrote.

Advertising thus grew as a faith-based initiative, with ad agencies and marketers alike believing it worked best when it raised awareness of brands and products across a large swath of a target population. In this "spray-and-pray" approach, success was based on gross ratings points (GRPs), print circulation, or total share of voice (SOV) achieved—in sharp contrast to any measure of advertising's true impact on consumer behavior. Volume of awareness was the highest value. "If 90 percent [of the audience] do not remember it," wrote Rosser Reeves, the leader of the giant Ted Bates ad agency, in 1960, at the peak of advertising's influence, "the story [of a particular advertisement] is not worn out."

With slowing economic growth during the 1970s, marketers started to reassess their laissez-faire attitude toward analyzing marketing effectiveness. But it wasn't until the 1990s and the rise of the Internet that the accountability revolution commenced. It was still in its infancy eight years ago, when then advertising columnist Randall Rothenberg (currently the CEO of the Interactive Advertising Bureau) wrote in *Wired* magazine: "New media technologies, by drastically reducing production and distribution costs and making possible almost continual and instantaneous refinements in message, promise to increase the efficiency of accountable advertising . . . The spurious distinction between image advertising and retail advertising will erode, then disappear, as each advertisement, every product placement, all editorial can be tied to transactions."

With that promise driving them, chief marketing officers (and their colleagues at every level of marketing organizations) will no longer be satisfied with campaigns that merely build awareness or consideration. They want campaigns that lead to action. More and more, they will insist on analysis and insight that can substantiate an ad's influence on consumer preference, purchase, and loyalty. They will push ad agencies and media companies to go beyond reach and frequency metrics to more tangible and quantifiable evidence of returns on marketing investment. No longer will marketers ask, "What is the cost of the GRPs I am buying?" Instead, they will want to know, "How many online registrations did that ad generate . . . and how many were converted into leads or actual sales?"

The Super CMOs are also pushing advertising innovation. They are not content to wait for their vendors to catch up to their needs. Instead, they are building new capabilities, both in-house and by fashioning new constellations of relationships with media companies and other marketing-services specialists.

Witness Procter & Gamble's Tremor, an in-house word-of-mouth marketing unit that fosters brand trial and consideration through a digital network of some 250,000 trend-setting teens. Interactive communities like Tremor tap into the power of "alpha consumers" (trendsetters and early adopters) to create multiple benefits for marketers. The sites generate buzz for new products by reaching key influencers; they bypass traditional media to connect with hard-to-engage segments (such as multitasking teens); they communicate brand messages in ways that consumers interpret as more authentic; and they deliver deep (most often proprietary) consumer insights. And they, too, can become revenue-generating assets in their own right. Blue-chip companies such as Coca-Cola, Toyota, and EMI have all been reported to have "rented" Tremor as part of their own teen-focused marketing efforts.

WHERE WE WERE . . . AND WHERE WE'RE GOING

Unfortunately, the new Super CMOs are still more the exception than the rule. To fully understand the ways in which marketing teams will change during the next few years, we first need to look back in time—to the marketing era that followed the popularization of television.

Commercial television had appeared in most of the United States and Europe by 1954. Since then, most marketing careers have followed well-trodden paths. New university graduates with liberal arts or undergraduate business degrees trained for five or six years with one of a few major companies, such as Procter & Gamble, Unilever, or Coca-Cola. They gained broad cross-category marketing experience, often in an international context. Working with outside advertising agencies, they promoted their products and services through mass communications media on a fixed playing field where all competitors had equal access and largely on the basis of syndicated research, which, for a price, was also available to all.

In the course of this work, ambitious and talented marketing professionals learned to choose and integrate outside agencies into their teams, to interpret consumer insights from market research studies, and, using those insights, to leverage TV, print, radio, and promotional programs to build a brand. Thus seasoned, in their thirties they became brand managers. In their forties, they became general managers—or they leapt to the "agency side." This generic career path established an industrywide pattern: specialized grooming for a role with familiar story lines and a well-worn plot.

It was a career trajectory that attracted people with energy and commitment, as well as a strong focus on action, results, and achievement. But, for the most part, it did not attract or nurture abstract thinkers. Twentieth-century marketers tended to prefer the detail and structure of the tried and true to the ambiguities and uncertainties of the new. They wanted—and knew how—to get things done, and their goal was to *manufacture* marketing as efficiently and as uniformly as their companies manufactured goods.

During all this time, television and brand management held sway over marketing theory and practice. It was all based on a judicious blending of media advertising, direct mail, and promotions, supervised by managers trained to analyze and make decisions on measurements of magnitude (i.e., the size of the audience reached). These managers were abetted by sets of contractors skilled, by turns, in advertising art and research science. In the last decade or so, most modern marketers added a pinch of the Internet, a sprinkle of product sampling, and a dash of PR, but the basic model remained largely unchanged. This skill set no longer suits the twenty-first-century marketer. Today, marketers need to know how to develop effective brand strategies in a world where communication options are growing exponentially. They have a vast array of new tools at their disposal—online video, blogs, interactive TV, mobile communication, and video games, to name just a few—that enable them to talk to consumers, to learn from them, and to market to them. But these tools have yet to be mastered. Those who have the foresight to experiment with new advertising platforms and sources of consumer insight, and those who have the know-how to scale that innovation into a more powerful marketing mix, will be at a premium.

The new generation of marketing leaders will have to choose between investing in a music download site or a campaign that makes use of mobile messaging, or between executing a lavish network TV buy or sponsoring a new video-on-demand service. And here's the challenge: as yet, nobody really knows how to make all of these decisions with consistent success.

Determining the best marketing mix for any brand will require a great deal of experimentation, networking, innovation, analytics, and risk taking—qualities associated more with start-ups and smaller companies than with the major marketers, and qualities that have never been adequately nurtured in a marketer's traditional career path.

As a result, major marketing companies are engaged in a worldwide hunt for skills, insight, and the combined analytic and creative power needed to make the most of this new media and advertising environment. Explains Carol Kruse, who became Coca-Cola's global interactive chief in the summer of 2007:

> We know there's a shortage of interactive marketing talent. We're looking around globally to see where we can leverage talent. In emerging technology areas, one country can be a year or three ahead of another. And we can use those experts to train the trainers or the other interactive folks or lead programs out of a region.

Of course, most contemporary marketers do not have the global resources of Coca-Cola. Nor are they accustomed to shaping, producing, and directly overseeing the media in which they place advertising. Yet those are among the skills that are most needed today.

Just as Procter & Gamble was active in the design and development of early TV programming, marketers in this current period of advertising flux must imagine, create, and finance new kinds of digital or interactive media and other innovative forms of marketing they engender. These marketers are working inside consumer goods and service companies, not for ancillary suppliers. They will invent the new programs and formats that will be for them what soaps and sitcoms were for earlier generations of marketers: compelling vehicles for capturing consumers' attention and for building brands.

HOW MARKETING NEEDS TO CHANGE

The transformation of media and advertising has profound implications for the way in which marketing is organized, for the skills and outlook required of professional marketers, and for the types of training they will need. Some key ingredients of the new model for marketing are already becoming clear.

More Media Savvy and Stronger Analytics

In a world with so many more advertising choices, marketers need to understand how different media, especially in digital form, can communicate their brand messages to consumers. With media emerging and changing so rapidly, they cannot simply rely on agency advice; marketers need to know how to ask the right questions and when to challenge their partners. Simultaneously, marketers must expand and refine their approaches to ROI analytics, brand metrics, and marketing mix modeling to take full advantage of the data and insight available from digital media.

Increased Entrepreneurship and Advertising Innovation

Marketers no longer can select and purchase proven instruments: they must envisage, shape, and develop new

17

tools for creating more effective consumer connections. This demands openness to experimentation, an inclination toward pioneering, and an ability to drive functional innovation in advertising and marketing as never before.

Integration Skills to Manage More Complex Partner Networks

To develop, deliver, and promote the emerging new forms of marketing and advertising, marketers will need to rethink and reconfigure their relationships to an ever broader range of partners—agencies, media companies, specialized providers, and consultants—to ensure that they get the best ideas and maximize their output. Marketers must also increase their investment in their own in-house creative, media planning, consumer insight, and other custom operations. There will be a premium for marketers who know how to orchestrate a fluid team with old participants (advertising agencies coming up to speed) and new ones (such as digital and interactive media specialists).

> We keep planning on the basis of campaigns, looking for short-term returns, using measurement systems that don't work. The real questions today are about how we can develop horizontal integrating processes and systems that work across disciplines, not just across communication formats. We need some new concepts and new approaches, not just rehashes of what we have been doing for the past 75 years.
> —Don E. Schultz, professor emeritus, Integrated Marketing Communications, Medill School of Journalism, Northwestern University.

More Effective Investment Approaches

Experimentation is a key to learning, but the "thousand points of light" approach to innovation often leads to the tyranny of small initiatives. Marketers must welcome new marketing and advertising opportunities in ways that create both greater effectiveness and increased speed to market and scale. In practice, this can mean either controlling investment funds from the center or setting clear portfoliowide marketing priorities (e.g., online video and social networks) and having business units share assets and infrastructure as well as learning.

Commitment to "Search and Reapply" Best Practices

Marketers must learn to capture all the benefits of multibrand and global portfolios. They must rigorously define the key success factors of high-impact campaigns and transfer that knowledge effectively across brands and/or geographies in the quest for speed and effectiveness in an always-on world. The key requirements: a common marketing vocabulary and set of performance metrics, an intellectual openness to sharing both strategies and results (both successes and failures), and the infrastructure and tools to communicate best practices across brands.

Ability to Educate Trade Partners and Other Constituents

As they make fundamental changes to their advertising and marketing efforts, marketers must proactively elicit

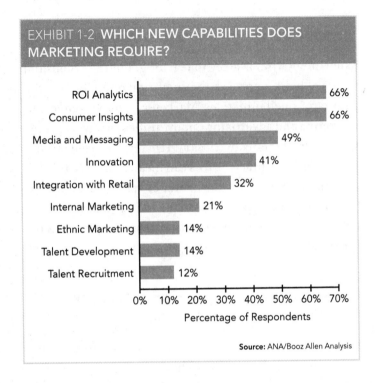

EXHIBIT 1-2 **WHICH NEW CAPABILITIES DOES MARKETING REQUIRE?**

Capability	Percentage
ROI Analytics	66%
Consumer Insights	66%
Media and Messaging	49%
Innovation	41%
Integration with Retail	32%
Internal Marketing	21%
Ethnic Marketing	14%
Talent Development	14%
Talent Recruitment	12%

Percentage of Respondents

Source: ANA/Booz Allen Analysis

the support of their trade partners and other constituents or risk losing their support. Some trade partners may not take a brand's efforts seriously unless they are supported by a major TV campaign. Others may not see how spending on nontraditional platforms (e.g., digital, word-of-mouth, PR, and the like) translates into success for *their* businesses. Marketers must explicitly and actively share their insights into how consumers' media usage affects brand affinity and, ultimately, sales.

In Exhibit 1-2, responses to an ongoing survey of marketing professionals by the Association of National Advertisers and Booz Allen Hamilton show a gap in perceived capabilities. The top two categories, in particular, focus on using analytics and consumer insight to improve marketing effectiveness: the great missing skill set for the future. The need for analytic skills, and the ability to gain customer insight from market data, will be particularly important. In the 1960s, advertising legend Bill Bernbach scornfully declared that "advertising is fundamentally persuasion, and persuasion happens to be not a science, but an art." Today, many marketing professionals still express disdain at the idea of advertising as a science rather than an art. They worry that their successors will be cousins to the math Ph.D.s who have long populated investment banks and the financial services industry. That won't happen in the same way. But today's disdain will be replaced by a more nuanced understanding of the marriage of art and algorithms.

The exploding availability of digitally driven consumer data has transformed marketing into a new frontier application for business mathematics. It is no wonder two-thirds of our senior marketers believe their greatest need is to develop capabilities in consumer insights and return on investment (ROI) analytics. Just as mathematics has revolutionized finance, it is reinvigorating marketing, as new models and algorithms extract value from consumer and business databases, enabling more precise targeting of messages to each consumer. Marketers will increasingly be called upon to make decisions that reflect broad marketing savvy and intimate awareness of the product's or service's current position in the marketplace. One of the new marketer's key skills will be the ability to marry fluency in higher mathematics and computer modeling to marketing flair and creativity. Search engine marketing (the development of better search engine positioning for promotional Web sites), for example, is just one of the most visible examples of the new fields of expertise that have become critical components for marketers, agencies, and media companies.

Those who have developed these skills and arrived at such metrics already are outperforming their rivals. These leaders are not just Internet powerhouses such as Google and Yahoo!; they include innovative number crunchers in retailing, finance, and other industries as well.

Meanwhile, the new emphasis on integration of the marketing value chain will not go away. In the short run, this reflects a disillusionment with the fragmentation that has come to characterize the marketing world. After decades of stability and growth, marketing has become subdivided into ever more finely granulated specialties, until the typical fast-moving consumer goods company orchestrates a web of suppliers that includes advertising agencies, buying agencies, creative specialists, direct-mail firms, and all manner of market researchers. This specialization has added responsiveness to the marketing-services system but also has added many layers of complexity.

In the long run, the call for integration reflects the evolving global business environment. Large and small companies alike will increasingly employ international marketing suppliers, often spread across several continents. They will make media buying decisions in local markets everywhere in the world. Supervising the huge extended enterprise required for global marketing is already a central skill for hundreds of thousands of men and women currently serving in marketing management roles.

Some of the giants of the marketing world have been the first to look beyond the current system to create new vehicles for integrated marketing supply chains. Strong retailers provide good examples. They are relatively new arrivals on the branding front lines, with much less vested in the traditional marketing system. They have found it natural to do much of their marketing themselves. Tesco, for example, bypasses large chunks of the conventional marketing services industry in the United Kingdom. It has brought its market research and analytics capability, which was formerly conducted by an independent firm, in house. Other retailers are reinventing media at the point of sale. Wal-Mart, for example, has made a major commitment to in-store TV, using video to create a potentially powerful connection to the consumer's shopping experience and "purchase" moment.

In traditional marketing teams, the action-oriented, authority-driven mindset still rules. This, too, will change. Indeed, too often it squeezes out the more innovative dispositions and the exploration and experimentation they bring. As the strategic agenda for marketers evolves, creative and commercial business-system perspectives will play a greater role in team composition so that companies can look up and down the value chain to imagine and experiment with new ways of operating. As marketing teams gain diversity and balance, team management—both internally and externally—in turn will become more integral to marketing and advertising effectiveness.

This might suggest that outsiders, in the form of small,

entrepreneurial upstart companies, are best positioned to effectively tear down and rebuild the media and marketing ecosystem. But the reality is that the big product marketers—whether they are in automotive products, consumer goods, technology, financial services, telecommunications, or travel—and the biggest product retailers are likely to be the leaders who reinvent the marketing model for the twenty-first century. Only they are big enough to take responsibility for marketing and advertising as a whole—and use their spending and size to reshape it. Their money and leverage will drive the whole marketing and media ecosystem.

These corporations also have the most direct and compelling need for the media and marketing ecosystem to perform well. Unlike the specialized suppliers, they don't have to answer to a single primary client. This means they are less constrained than other members of the system and are free to reassemble the pieces in new and interesting ways. And some of the best are leaders in using their freedom and power. The broader marketing strategies being pursued by such companies as Nike, Procter & Gamble, Capital One, GM, Tesco, Johnson & Johnson, and Coca-Cola are symptomatic of the direction that marketers across all industry sectors and geographies will take—they will pursue an agenda of global, consumer-focused, analytically rich innovation.

The winners will be enabled by their prescience, vigor, and determination in reshaping their marketing teams before their competitors do. That's the place for companies to start. New times call for new capabilities and for team structures that can win in an era of technology, uncertainty, and change.

PROSPECTS FOR MARKETING JOBS

In the United States alone, 664,000 people were serving in sales, marketing, advertising, promotions, and public relations management in 2004, the most recent year for which figures have been published by the U.S. Bureau of Labor Statistics. Broadcasting accounted for another 327,000 jobs. The motion picture and video industries contributed 368,000 more. The Bureau projected marketing-related occupations to rise in number by about 25 percent by 2012 and broadcast and media-related occupations to rise by about 20 percent.

Such projections inevitably reflect the job descriptions of the old marketing and media structures. Nonetheless, even taking into account the shifts in the industry, these labor projections may well be correct. The emergence of consumer markets around the world, and of digital media opportunities, suggests that thousands of marketing professionals will be needed in the future. The only caveat: their jobs probably won't bear much resemblance to those of their predecessors.

LEAVE THE PAST BEHIND

Museums are repositories of history, and much of the advertising and marketing from the twentieth century is ready for permanent enshrinement and display. As luck would have it, as we write this a new museum of advertising icons is preparing to open in Kansas City. It will be the perfect place for the Aflac duck, the Geico gecko, Tony the Tiger, and the Pillsbury Doughboy, along with a selection of celebrated 30-second Super Bowl spots, mass-audience TV diaries, and other relics of an industry that has already turned the corner into the future.

Does this mean gloom and doom for traditional marketers? Only if they refuse to change. In fact, there's never been as much potential for innovation or as much room for personal growth in marketing. (Advertising creatives: You think it's tough pulling together a 30-second commercial for network TV? How about a brilliant five-second spot for next year's Super Bowl that delivers measurable results before the next snap of the ball?)

What seems chaotic to some is dynamic to those who are willing to embrace the always-on environment. And winners—those who are working across the media and marketing ecosystem to create compelling consumer messaging and brand experiences—are emerging. Already, their work is more relevant, more interactive, and more results-oriented than ever before. The future of advertising and marketing will also be more exciting and challenging—for professionals and consumers alike.

RESOURCES

➤ *Advertising Age*, 100 Leading National Advertisers, 2005 and 2007.

➤ Borden, Neil H., *The Economic Effects of Advertising*, Irwin, Chicago, 1942.

➤ Harter, Gregor, Edward Landry, and Andrew Tipping, "The New Complete Marketer," *strategy + business*, autumn 2007.

➤ Hyde, Paul, Edward Landry, and Andrew Tipping, "Making the Perfect Marketer," *strategy + business*, winter 2004.

➤ Rawlinson, Richard, "Beyond Brand Management," *strategy + business*, summer 2006.

➤ For more resources and up-to-date information, see www.businessfuture.com.

2

MEDIAMORPHOSIS: THE CONSUMER IN CHARGE

THERE IS ONE overriding, simple, but powerful message for all twenty-first-century marketing, media, and advertising executives: insight about consumers is the currency that trumps all others. In just the last few years, major marketers—not to mention media companies and agencies—have come to realize that the ways in which consumers perceive and connect with brands have changed forever. Henceforth, only those marketers with smart, hard-working, and actionable insight will be able to connect with their consumers in the right place, at the right time, with the right message.

Or, to put it another way: "The power of the consumer affects how you market, how you develop products, how you change your launch time frames, and how you price things." That observation comes from Omid Kordestani, the senior vice president of global sales and business development at Google, Inc.

Companies have long paid homage to the consumer, of course, and to the importance of intimate knowledge of and connection with their customers. But most longtime marketers would concede that during the decades of mass media—from the introduction of commercial radio in the early 1920s to the release of the first World Wide Web browser in 1992—the practice of marketing was focused largely on selling mass products to mass audiences via mass media. This inevitably meant that consumers (even business-to-business customers) became, in marketers' eyes, research constructs—soulless aggregations of demographic data, viewed only through the one-way mirrors of focus-group facilities. Members of a targeted marketing segment—teenagers or working mothers, for instance—could be treated as a single group, often numbering in the millions.

This approach became so ingrained among marketers that it was essentially unconscious. It made their jobs much easier. However, it also led many marketers to reduce consumers to caricatures—even as marketing leaders routinely, but vainly, admonished them *not* to do so. "The consumer is not an idiot," advertising legend David Ogilvy famously wrote 45 years ago. "She is your wife."

And no one questioned the idea that marketers should control their interplay with customers—if only because it was hard to see any alternatives. There were only a finite number of television networks, magazines, newspapers, and radio stations; thus, the "shelf space" of media was limited, and nearly all of it was subsidized by advertising. There was no penalty for pushing broadcast-style communications that were more focused on the seller's business priorities than on consumers' real interests, as consumers had no choice but to pay attention. Where else could they turn for entertainment or information, especially at such a low cost?

But now, the media environment has changed in ways that place consumers irrevocably and permanently in control. That's the natural consequence of having myriad outbound communications channels, on the Web and elsewhere; a multitude of technologies that enable either ad skipping or outright ad blocking; an immense number of low-cost and amateur content providers; and a rich variety of on-demand and portable media available on devices ranging from a wall-sized flat screen to a pocket-sized iPhone.

During the five years between 2001 and 2006, consumers dramatically shifted their media habits, as shown in Exhibit 2-1. For instance, they reduced the amount of time they spent with music, broadcast TV, and newspapers by more than 10 percent, and they increased the amount of time they spent on the Internet fourfold and the amount of time they spent on mobile devices more than tenfold. Those trends are continuing, giving the mobile phone and the Web—both of which will allow consumers far more control over their media experience—an even greater presence in most people's lives during the years to come.

In this type of media environment, marketers can no longer win simply through interruption. Consumers have been freed; they no longer have to sit through commercials to get the content they want. And there is ample evidence that they are tuning out advertising. Studies by Forrester

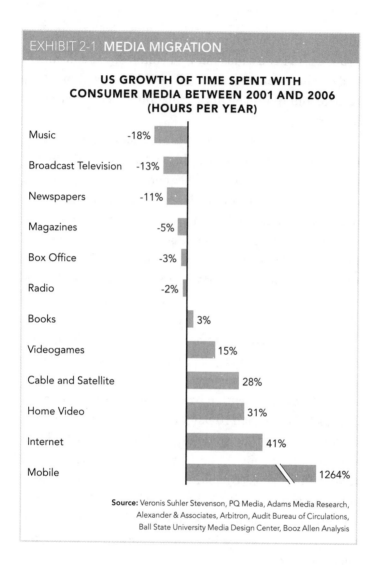

EXHIBIT 2-1 **MEDIA MIGRATION**

US GROWTH OF TIME SPENT WITH CONSUMER MEDIA BETWEEN 2001 AND 2006 (HOURS PER YEAR)

Music	-18%
Broadcast Television	-13%
Newspapers	-11%
Magazines	-5%
Box Office	-3%
Radio	-2%
Books	3%
Videogames	15%
Cable and Satellite	28%
Home Video	31%
Internet	41%
Mobile	1264%

Source: Veronis Suhler Stevenson, PQ Media, Adams Media Research, Alexander & Associates, Arbitron, Audit Bureau of Circulations, Ball State University Media Design Center, Booz Allen Analysis

Research, Yankelovich, and others show widespread adoption of many media-manipulation devices—digital video recorders (DVRs), MP3 music players, satellite radios, banner blockers, and the like—specifically for the purpose of advertising control.

In addition, it is unusual for a marketer to be able to capture the full attention of a consumer today through just one medium. Consumers have more media at their disposal than ever before. In an always-on age of digital recorders, online video, and mobile devices, and with most young consumers being accustomed to playing video games, instant messaging (IMing), and watching television all at the same time, marketers have to assume that even if they've produced a compelling message for one platform, the consumer's attention is most likely fixed on a different one. Media multitasking is so prevalent that it has provoked a round of academic studies to gauge its impact on education; as the Kaiser Family Foundation pointed out, "Two decades ago, it was not unusual to see a young person read while listening to music. . . . But the computer promotes multitasking [in unprecedented ways], providing natural breaks in work (download times, etc.) and regular interruptions (instant message pop-up screens). Hence, today's youth, who have grown up with computers, are perhaps more prone to media multitasking."

Television retains a powerful pull on younger audiences, even in the Internet age; but it isn't an exclusive pull. No one devotes his or her full attention to just TV or a newspaper anymore. More typical is a multitasking teenager—sitting in front of the tube, playing video games, reading a magazine, and checking in with an IM universe, all while doing homework, as shown in Exhibit 2-2.

Some statistics:

> While watching TV, 74 percent of people read a newspaper and 66 percent go online.

> While reading a magazine, 59 percent watch TV.

EXHIBIT 2-2 **LEARNING TO REACH A MULTITASKING AUDIENCE**

Photograph by Image Source Black. Courtesy of Getty Images.

> While reading newspapers, 52 percent watch TV, and 50 percent listen to the radio.

"The 30-second commercial isn't what it used to be, because television watchers now multitask," says Cie Nicholson, Pepsi-Cola North America's chief marketing officer. "They're on the Internet and their cell phones at the same time they're in front of their TVs. So while the number of television hours watched may have risen, people are no longer watching passively."

In this new world, the old marketing models are rapidly declining in value, and many of them are already obsolete. "Consumers" can no longer be treated as statistical abstractions. They must now be recognized as infinitely varied individuals with measurable preferences and actions. Moreover, they are rejecting the information, entertainment, and marketing communications that they find irrelevant, and exercising their option to opt in to those media that give them more of what *they* want: greater personalization, relevance, and interactivity. This makes them an entirely different kind of advertising target. They are no longer passive and conveniently available; instead, they are selective, skeptical, and demanding. The power in the marketing relationship has shifted to them.

Hence the painful challenge facing top executives in marketing and media right now: to reinvent their profession as a consumer-centered craft. As more and more consumers ignore (and actively avoid) commodity advertising, *engagement*, *relevance*, and *results* are becoming the focus of marketing energy and creativity. If David Ogilvy were alive today, no doubt he'd be saying, "The consumer is not an idiot; she is your boss."

FROM IMPRESSIONS TO RELEVANCE

Because the consumer is the new boss in the media marketplace, insight into his or her behavior and preferences—the perspective that can make advertising relevant—has become far too strategically important to depend on the research methods of the past. The mechanistic market research methods of the mass-market age and the generic overviews that third-party providers of syndicated research supply to brand managers are simply not enough. Instead, successful marketers are building their own stores of consumer insight bit by bit, by finding systematic ways to inform their judgment through sustained, scaled-up exposure to what consumers are actually thinking, experiencing, and telling one another.

The first companies to deal with this new reality have been some of the most farsighted consumer products manufacturers, and they are setting the pace for change—starting with their own practices. "Our people are evolving along with this changing media model," says PepsiCo's Nicholson. "We do a lot more grassroots work now. We've always done sampling, but when we bought SoBe Beverages in 2001, it brought us tremendous expertise in that area. We've also gained sophistication in the digital arena and in customer marketing, and our innovation skills have improved as well."

In an always-on world in which media usage is migrating to digital, advertising can be blocked or skipped, and content can be consumed on demand, marketers have to find new ways to distinguish between those aspects of consumer behavior that will remain the same and those that will change. Many are turning to direct observation of and contact with consumers.

At Yahoo!, for example, senior executives go into in-house laboratories once a month to interview consumers directly. "I want to continue to build empathy," said Cammie Dunaway, during her tenure as Yahoo!'s chief marketing officer, "for what consumers are going through and create an appreciation for the value of talking to consumers." (Dunaway has since left to become executive vice president of sales and marketing for Nintendo of America.) Among the discoveries: that in many cases, online users don't pay attention to the latest and greatest features that the company's engineers are serving up. Indeed, they find those features unnecessary or even frustrating. This, of course, has been a perennial problem in many technology companies. Today, however, if the companies can maintain a dialogue with consumers about their needs and preferences, those pitfalls can be avoided. As they realize the value of having the most informed consumer insight, marketers, agencies, and media companies will engage in fierce competition for this advantage. For the moment, marketers have established a significant lead over both media companies and advertising agencies in this crucial game. Over the last few years, marketers have made massive investments in new research techniques, database marketing, and customer relationship management. They have also expanded their participation in digital media, in-store marketing, word-of-mouth marketing, and experiential marketing—powerful tools that are not only key elements of tomorrow's high-impact marketing and media mix, but also critically important vehicles for generating consumer insight.

Technology allows marketers to give consumers a voice. And that's a dramatic and powerful change, as long as we pay attention to what our customers are saying, In the [twentieth century], we did monologue marketing. We did most—if not all—of the talking. And we expected the consumer to listen. Now, in the twenty-first century, we've moved to a dialogue. Consumers want to be heard. In fact, they will not tolerate not being heard.

—John Hayes, chief marketing officer, American Express.

In-depth market insight—into who consumers are, what they want, and what they will actually buy—is not achievable at scale from traditional sources of market and audience research. But it *can* be discovered in digital media, where marketers can more easily listen in on what their consumers are saying and doing every day. For marketers, digital is creating many new opportunities to hear the voice of their consumer. Search engines, social networks, blogs, video exchanges, commerce sites, content destinations, games, and other interactive media are poised to become valuable new sources of consumer insight for marketers. Indeed, the most difficult challenge is not developing those channels, but knowing how to prioritize them: determining which truly offer a unique line of sight into consumer needs as opposed to just adding more noise.

DATA AND TOUCHPOINTS EVERYWHERE

Why is the digital experience such an appealing source of consumer insight for marketers? Because of the expanding ability to capture measurable data almost everywhere consumers go. Once issues involving data access and privacy are resolved, records of clicks on Web sites and data captured in cookies (tracking files that are maintained by a computer's Web browser) can provide marketers with the electronic equivalent of fingerprints to trace every aspect of a consumer's online experience. These fingerprints include records of sites visited, videos watched or sent to friends, topics searched, and products recommended or, even better, purchased. When these are combined with the volunteered "opt-in" information that consumers provide about themselves, the result is a rich consumer profile that can be used to better inform every aspect of marketing. Just as important, the clickstream data are two-way and serve, for the first time, as a census of actual consumer activity—far more valuable than projections derived from samples of analog media usage.

In traditional media, an advertiser buys an audience based on an *estimate* of how many impressions are created among a particular demographic, such as the number of 18- to 49-year-olds who watch NBC's *Heroes*. That number, in turn, is reflected in a cost-per-thousand-impressions (CPM) price tag. In online media, marketers can similarly buy inventory based on the same CPM model. But they can also satisfy their thirst for accountability by paying based on measures that are directly related to actual consumer activity. They can buy cost per click (CPC), where value is based on how many times consumers click on an ad, or cost per action (CPA), where value is based on sales or registrations or any other action that the marketer cares to specify.

Furthermore, online marketers increasingly can place and buy their advertising based on actual insights into consumer interests, rather than target demographics. When PepsiCo launched a digital campaign in 2007 in support of Aquafina Alive, a vitamin-enhanced water, it concentrated its advertising on approximately 4,000 Web sites that Pepsi knew delivered a heavy concentration of consumers interested in "healthy lifestyles." This focus on interests— as opposed to demographics such as "upscale women"— led to a 300 percent improvement in click-through.

"We've never been able to get to this level of granularity," commented John Vail, Pepsi's director of the interactive marketing group, to the *Wall Street Journal*.

The availability of more and more granular data can, of course, be daunting. Marketers, media companies, and agencies will thus need to learn to analyze the brand and relationship-building value of different usage occasions. These are the *touchpoints*—the media platforms where consumers connect to brands.

The starting point for determining the touchpoints that matter the most is drawing maps of the target consumer's media behavior. These diagrams are compiled through detailed analysis of key consumer segments. The analyses highlight where and when the individuals come into contact with media or entertainment: at home, at work, or on the go. The maps reveal which platforms (television, mobile phones, iPods, PDAs), media (TV shows, blogs, video games, social networks, instant messaging), and brands are preferred. They also track the occasions (after school, weekends, morning commute) and frequency of each of these activities. Many go a step further and link these insights to nonmedia touchpoints, such as shopping habits or experiences with customer service. These maps are used to determine where the best opportunities exist to create a brand connection that is relevant and that can affect consumer behavior.

The touchpoint mapping process is then replicated across different target segments and brands. For instance, people who are just getting to know a brand may have one touchpoint, perhaps through a visit to a local retailer. Brand loyalists may have another—they may be regularly checking an online forum. Heavy users of a competitor's products may have a third, such as word of mouth from friends or, getting back to basics, a network TV campaign.

The insights that come from mapping touchpoints enable marketers to think more effectively about different consumer segments, to determine whether advertising should be entertaining or informational, and to identify which media platforms can most effectively move consumers from awareness to purchase.

JPMorgan Chase used a touchpoint-based insight in 2006 when it chose Facebook, the popular social utility Web site, to introduce a new credit card named +1 to college students. "We felt Facebook would be a good partner for us, since they had such strong credibility in the students' world," explained Sangeeta Prasad, who oversees branding for Chase Card Services. Students don't see credit-card issuers or financial institutions in general as meeting their needs." Chase promoted the card with a sponsored Facebook group that attracted nearly 34,000 members in a year. "This puts [that Facebook group] in the upper ranks of the 190 or so 'sponsored' groups, in the company of American Eagle and the Dave Matthews Band Summer Tour," reported the *New York Times*. Exhibit 2-3 shows how this Facebook page based on touchpoint research created marketing relevance for the +1 credit card. Relevance was built by the Facebook presence and by the restriction of group membership to college students. As Chase and other companies gain experience with social networking, sites will become more sophisticated—in content, in look and feel, and in their ability to track and analyze consumer behavior.

The ability to use online media to *know* what will be relevant to consumers, rather than *guesstimating*, repre-

EXHIBIT 2-3 CHASE'S FACEBOOK GROUP

Facebook is a registered trademark of Facebook, Inc.

sents a significant paradigm shift in marketing. It may be the antidote to the loss of control that many people in media, advertising, and marketing currently feel. Marketers will never again dominate consumers the way they once did. But they can use this deeper, more informed data-driven analysis to become partners with consumers. They can thus create the kinds of advertising and media experiences that will strengthen their brands in the long run.

A BETTER VIEW OF THE CONSUMER

With more touchpoints, granular data, and insight, marketers have more opportunities than ever to listen and

MATCHING MESSAGES TO MEDIA

Deeper consumer insights naturally lead to a more sophisticated media mix. Marketers are realizing that even if the choice of medium isn't the whole message, it is an integral part of the message. Here are a few of the ways in which different media support varying marketing objectives:

➤ **Communicating functional or emotional benefits.** Video content (TV or digital) can tell a story, bring a brand to life visually, and build awareness.

➤ **Delivering brand and product information.** Print and online channels create unique opportunities to go deep with consumers, building in-depth knowledge in fields ranging from home improvement to pharmaceuticals, strengthening brand credibility, and ultimately generating brand advocacy and loyalty.

➤ **Driving purchases and trials.** Retail promotion, shelf placement, packaging, sampling, and in-store media can all change consumers' minds—where and when they are ready to buy.

➤ **Connecting on the go.** Outdoor and other place-based media can capture consumers' attention outside the home, reaching them in less cluttered media environments.

➤ **Creating a brand experience.** Experiential marketing creates an environment that enables a brand to connect directly with consumers' interests and passions through real-world events and online experiences.

respond to consumers in an informed, integrated, and relevant manner. Procter & Gamble was one of the first major companies to realize this and to reorient itself toward the consumer. P&G's marketers learned to talk *with* consumers, instead of talking *at* them. The company, in turn, has developed a model of persuasion based on consumer understanding, advertising relevance, and magnetic attraction, thus creating the kind of marketing that would naturally draw people in.

"We learned to value the heart as well as the mind," says Jim Stengel, the company's global marketing officer. "We've typically been a very rational company, very data-based. This isn't something we want to lose. But we became more empathetic, more of a listening company than we ever had been."

One great example is the company's new approach to disposable diapers. As Stengel notes, the learning process for market positioning began not in a boardroom, with backroom number crunchers, or in highly structured focus groups, but in open conversations with the company's consumers. "We spent half a day at one of our quarterly top management meetings with very media-savvy moms. We wanted our senior people, who are digital immigrants, to understand how people are spending their time and getting their information. After four or five hours of an experience like that, you can't come back and say, 'Well, we're going to do a media plan that is 95 percent TV.' You think about things differently."

This was a leap for the company that had created the first commercially successful disposable diaper and thus invented the category. For years, the brand had been based on functional benefits. "There are fewer wet bottoms in the world because of us," Stengel explains. "And we had an entire R&D organization focused on fluid absorption, its speed, [its effect on] skin health, and so on." But after listening in depth to customers, the marketers realized that mothers were looking for something beyond containment and dryness; they were looking for products that would help their babies develop and mature.

"That really made us think about where we wanted to be, and how moms saw us. We said, 'Don't we aspire to be that baby care leader, and really make a key difference with moms and babies?'" Shifting the brand message from dryness to baby development was a major undertaking, going far beyond the marketing department: P&G had hundreds of R&D people and plants with tens of millions of dollars invested. All of this had to be adapted to address a new set of needs. "Babies wear a diaper 24/7 for almost three years," Stengel points out. "It needs to be soft and comfortable like clothing and have a design that goes hand in hand with overall performance and consumer satisfaction. Everything starts to change."

Sometimes, the greatest hurdle in assimilating this type of customer insight is getting the organization to pay attention. "In the initial days," Stengel continues, "people thought we were nuts. How can a diaper help in a baby's development? But actually, when you start to think about it, it starts to orient R&D to say, 'How can we help babies sleep better?' Why are we concerned about babies sleeping better? Because sleep is important to brain development. It helps relationship skills. Thinking like that, and decisions made like that, compounded, have a big effect on a business, and on the way we're able to help improve life for our consumers."

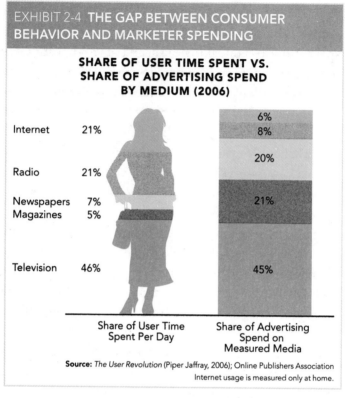

EXHIBIT 2-4 **THE GAP BETWEEN CONSUMER BEHAVIOR AND MARKETER SPENDING**

SHARE OF USER TIME SPENT VS. SHARE OF ADVERTISING SPEND BY MEDIUM (2006)

Internet	21%	6%
		8%
		20%
Radio	21%	
Newspapers	7%	21%
Magazines	5%	
Television	46%	45%

Share of User Time Spent Per Day | Share of Advertising Spend on Measured Media

Source: *The User Revolution* (Piper Jaffray, 2006); Online Publishers Association Internet usage is measured only at home.

This kind of fundamental reassessment of a product is in itself a major challenge. Now consider the challenge of creating that same kind of deep customer intimacy across a portfolio of global product lines. It's a nearly impossible assignment using analog media and traditional market research alone. The desired endgame becomes achievable only when a company's advertising energy shifts toward the kinds of engaging and relevant messaging and experiences—more often found today in digital—that trigger consumer conversation.

Big companies are often slow to react to change, and here's the proof: advertising spending in the United States does not yet reflect the contemporary media rituals of the U.S. consumer. As marketers catch up to these new patterns of media consumption, the bar charts in Exhibit 2-4 can be expected to align more closely as corporate advertising budgets allocated to newspapers, broadcast television, and magazines shift further toward Internet spending. The bottom line for marketers and media companies is that the current gap between online usage (~21 percent) and online spending (~6 to 8 percent) is too great, especially given the ongoing advancements in online technology and targeting, the increased availability of consumer and professional media online, the growing online sophistication of marketers and consumers, and the potential for greater accountability and ROI via digital media versus more traditional platforms.

In some international markets where online usage is especially high, this realignment of the marketing mix is happening at an even more accelerated rate. Take for example the United Kingdom, where online captured about 15 percent of all measured media spending in 2007 (compared to about 8 percent in the United States). Here, WPP's Group M is forecasting that by the end of 2008, online spending will represent 24.8 percent of all advertising spending versus a forecasted 26.0 percent share for television. Group M anticipates similar changes in the advertising mix in markets such as Sweden and Denmark where TV and print are equally vulnerable to the advances of online advertising.

While there are some unique aspects of these markets (e.g., the large presence of public broadcasters such as the BBC depresses the size of the overall commercial TV spend, and they skew even more greatly toward print than U.S. broadcasters), they do represent what can happen

EXHIBIT 2-5 U.S. AD SPENDING BY MEDIUM

($)	2006 U.S. Ad Spend (Billions)	Households (Millions)	Ad Spend/ Household
Promotions	$111	112	$993
Direct Telephone	$104	112	$929
Newspapers	$49	56	$885
Direct Mail	$60	112	$537
Broadcast Television	$48	109	$444
Cable Television	$24	75	$318
Magazines	$24	86	$279
Internet/Online	$17	75	$224
Radio	$22	110	$196
Yellow Pages	$15	112	$137
Outdoor	$7	112	$61
Average			$455

**Internet = $224 per Home
vs. $444 for Broadcast Television vs. $885 for Newspapers**

Note: Promotions includes incentives, promotional products, point-of-purchase, specialty printing, coupons, premiums, promotional licensing, promotional fulfillment, product sampling, and in-store marketing

Source: Morgan Stanley, Veronis Schuler Stevenson, eMarketer, Newspaper Association of America, Television Bureau of Advertising, Magazine Publishers of America, Publishers Information Bureau, Interactive Advertising Bureau, National Cable & Telecommunication Association, Radio Advertising Bureau, Outdoor Advertising Association of America, Booz Allen analysis

when marketers set a more aggressive advertising and media agenda, pushing their agencies for more innovative campaigns and working directly in concert with their media partners. As illustrated in Exhibit 2-5, online in the United States is already capturing more on an average household basis than such long established media offerings as radio, yellow pages, and outdoor, and it has been taking share from other media—first print and now, increasingly, television. With roughly 8 out of 10 Americans reportedly online every day, it is not too big a leap to expect that online's average spend per household (currently about $455) will continue to increase, especially given the potential to capture even greater share gains from newspapers, magazines, and television as well as from below-the-line offerings such as promotions and direct mail/telephone as that spending transitions to digital as well.

PIONEERS IN CONSUMER-CENTRIC STRATEGY

With so many options available to marketers for reaching consumers, there is no one dominant approach to translating a brand into a compelling message or experience. It requires relentless experimentation and the courage to stretch, morph, and integrate campaigns across traditional media, digital media, and even retail. This intricate mosaic of marketing bits and pieces stands in sharp contrast to the budget-busting fireworks of the TV-centric Super Bowl showcase approach.

Again, Procter & Gamble exemplifies the successful digital-age pioneer. The world's largest advertiser has been actively tinkering with its marketing mix to determine which communication channels work best for its brands. These efforts have been promising enough for CEO A. G. Lafley to proclaim, "If you step back and look at our [marketing] mix across most of the major brands, it's clearly shifting, and it's shifting from measured media to in-store, to the Internet and to trial activity." Nor is P&G alone; more and more consumer product advertising spending will be going toward digital content, e-newsletters, branded entertainment, and viral/word-of-mouth programs, along with a greater overall focus on in-store programs.

Since launching its Web site homemadesimple.com in 2000, P&G has demonstrated some of the new ways in which packaged goods companies can benefit from the digital environment. Home Made Simple is to the Internet what soap operas were to television: a model for what can happen when a marketer becomes a digital publisher. The site is a branded destination with a distinct identity (P&G's corporate name is evident only to those who look carefully for it), scaling across an entire product category, and designed to create a valuable direct-to-consumer touchpoint. The site focuses on P&G's home-care portfolio, including brands such as Swiffer, Cascade, Dawn, Tide, Mr. Clean, and Febreze. Its electronic pages are replete with contextually relevant content—product information, community stories, household ideas (recipes, decorating, tips for storing antiques, etc.), sweepstakes, promotions, and even music by the likes of Diana Krall and Harry Connick, Jr. Exhibit 2-6 shows the site in late 2007. As the exhibit shows, this site is welcoming and informative. It attracts target consumers and leads them to brand loyalty for P&G's products.

Home Made Simple's value goes well beyond its Web presence. For P&G, it is a powerful relationship marketing vehicle with more than six million monthly e-newsletter subscribers. And more recently, the site itself has become a multimedia brand with a weekly presence on the Discovery Network's TLC.

Similarly, P&G's Beinggirl.com is a digital destination for teenage girls that was developed to create a relevant online environment for brands such as Secret, Cover Girl, Always, and Tampax. Here again, the value of listening to consumers has paid dividends for P&G. Initially, Beinggirl's content was predominantly educational—neither especially exciting nor fun. But by asking the site's users

EXHIBIT 2-6 **HOME MADE SIMPLE: A DIGITAL CUSTOMER TOUCHPOINT**

H💠ME | simple solutions for easy living
made simple

search home made simple [ ] [search]

| organized**life** | celebrate**living** | clever**kitchen** | outside**pleasures** | easy**décor** |

naturally artistic

Bring pieces of nature inside to create beautiful decorations.

Bringing the outside in is something that many people do when they decorate in their homes. And that often means bringing in live plants and flowers. But here's another way to beautifully and inexpensively bring the outside in: create artistic sculptural arrangements with bare branches for a striking and simple new look.

easy**décor**

send this to a friend ✉

Decorating with branches from your neighborhood is awfully simple and inexpensive, but this look is also very popular. When coupled with a slim glass vase, this is a natural yet modern decorating technique.

Refreshing Walk for A Fresh New Look

Start this décor project by going for a walk. Go into your back yard, into a park or just for a walk around the block, keeping your eye out for pieces of wood on the ground. Look for interesting textures and shapes in branches. Sticks that have interesting angles or take unexpected turns are what you want—something that's going to create some visual intrigue.

To receive great articles like this every month, **sign up for our FREE Newsletter today!** ▸

Wishbones, curls and right angles can be among the pieces that'll look great. Long, strong branches work best, but go for a variety of lengths. Of course, keep in mind where you're going to be putting them in your home.

Presentation Ready

Home Buzz in the **Home Made Simple Community** at KomJunction

Zucchini salad recipe... 🔊
jenniferj

Make your own herb garden... 🔊
amandabrown

[visit the community ▸]

Wash your branches with dish liquid and water. Be careful not to strip them clean of their bark. Just clean them enough to remove the dirt and grime on the wood. If you have a hose outside, you may find it easier to clean outdoors than in your sink.

Let the branches dry on a towel. As they're drying, take a look at them and start thinking about how you want to arrange them.

Artistic Arrangement

Arrange your branches in a large, glass vase, at least 20 to 30 inches high and 8 to 12 inches wide. It needs to be big enough to support the weight of the branches and keep them from toppling over. Take the largest, heaviest piece and place it in the vase first. This will be the visual anchor of the arrangement. Get it in place first, then arrange all of the other pieces around it.

Add in a few of the smaller, simpler branches until you like how it's starting to look. Take a step back and admire your work. Notice how your eyes follow the lines of the arrangement and adjust the branches to create a balanced and artistic arrangement.

Another, even easier arrangement uses a single branch. Find one beautiful branch, with lovely texture and a whimsical shape, about 30 inches long. Place it in a fishbowl at an angle and you have a graceful and simple sculpture. If using a clear vase, consider adding wooden, glass or stone beads for additional visual interest. This will also add weight and stability to help prevent toppling.

Versatile Décor Accessory

Now decide where you're going to put your arrangement. Because the piece is simple and inviting, it should match many of the styles you've already used in your interior décor. This arrangement looks beautiful as a centerpiece, or on a side table or credenza in any living area. Place it on your kitchen island to create height and interest. Smaller versions can look great in a bathroom or hallway.

In fact, this arrangement is so versatile and pretty that you may want to keep it year round and move it to different spots in your home each season. And it is simple and inexpensive to update with

New Bonus Clips!
View exclusive clips from our TV show
your guide to Home Made Simple TV

neat**net** + **notable**
Mr. Clean® now with Febreze® freshness
view article

great**giveaways**
Enter the It Only Takes One Sweepstakes
view all sweepstakes

special**something** 'or your money back'
Featured article:
Dawn® Direct Foam™ ♥me!
view all articles

EXHIBIT 2-7 GROUNDS FOR VIRAL MARKETING

what kind of content they wanted, P&G learned that music was high on their list. The consumer products company then enlisted Sony BMG, which brought new music offerings to the site. Today, Beinggirl.com connects P&G directly to about 500,000 teenage girls each month.

P&G's belief that small numbers of highly motivated consumers can become big multipliers has pushed the company to the forefront of viral and word-of-mouth marketing. Because it's difficult to sell coffee to younger consumers through traditional media, P&G's Folgers experimented with a viral campaign of video clips distributed on such Web sites as adcritic.com, boardsmag.com, buzzpatrol.com, and YouTube.com. The Folgers commercial shown in Exhibit 2-7, released in 2007, has entered the awareness of young consumers through deliberate viral marketing on sites like YouTube. P&G's Tremor

(250,000 teens) and Vocalpoint (600,000 moms) units are two additional examples of the word-of-mouth marketing capabilities the company has developed as alternatives to traditional media.

What do all of these different elements add up to? For P&G, the answer is a reduced reliance on traditional media. A further result is a multitiered strategy of establishing and nurturing a direct-to-consumer relationship. P&G's long-term goal is to create a relationship marketing capability that can directly address 40 to 60 million households—a scale that would have been unimaginable in the predigital marketing universe. Furthermore, the flexibility of digital media enables P&G to pursue more rapid executions and adjustments in its advertising, marketing, and promotions, which in turn yield more unfiltered consumer feedback and granular insight. Just a decade ago, findings from bulky focus groups would later be synthesized and fed back into another forum. Now, refinements in marketing efforts can be made almost in real time on digital media. And the lessons learned from these experiences have the potential to inform decisions across many elements of the corporate value chain: product development, manufacturing, retail distribution, and, of course, advertising.

ONLINE MARKET RESEARCH

These shifts represent a future of marketing and advertising that is grounded in an up-to-the-minute, real-time view of consumers. To forecast what twenty-first-century consumers will want, marketers are actively pursuing new research techniques and pushing their trade, agency, and media partners to provide the most compelling insights possible into *their* specific marketing targets.

Toward this end, some leading marketers (General Mills, Kraft Foods, and Charles Schwab & Co., to name three) have discovered that private online communities—the equivalent of exclusive social networks—can help them connect more deeply with their best consumers. The value of this depth of connection: a pipeline into consumer insight that is effectively always on, exclusive learning from the field, and more rapid and interactive implementations than were ever available from traditional research methods.

"Everybody is talking about communities now, and so the question is no longer 'Should we have one?' but more 'What kind should it be?' and 'How can we design it to truly engage customers?'" says Diane Hessan, CEO of Communispace, Inc., a Watertown, Massachusetts—based marketing services firm that specializes in creating online communities for major corporations.

SOCIAL NETWORKING: WHAT WORKS?

Founded in 1999, Communispace has created more than 250 custom online communities for the likes of Kraft, Hewlett-Packard, Charles Schwab, Hallmark, Unilever, GlaxoSmithKline, Hilton Hotels, General Mills, PepsiCo, and Capital One. Not long ago, the company studied the behavior of more than 26,500 members of more than 66 private online communities to determine the vitality of these digital retreats. Here are a few of the findings:

➤ *Intimacy breeds participation.* A full 86 percent of the people who log on to private communities (average size: 300 to 500 people) were active contributors. They posted comments, started and joined dialogues, brainstormed ideas, and shared photos, among other actions. Only 14 percent logged in and "lurked." By contrast, the ratio is reversed on public social networking Web sites. This disparity suggests that the more intimate the setting, the more consumer participation and involvement marketers can expect.

➤ *Familiarity is a powerful driver.* While the contribution and lurker rates were fairly consistent between branded and unbranded sites, branded sites had a higher volume of participation.

➤ *Men and women respond differently.* More women participated than men. But once men joined in, they participated with slightly greater frequency—4.8 weekly contributions for men compared to 4.1 for women.

➤ *Homogeneity triggers participation.* Communities built on specific demographics have higher participation rates. Women and men participated more in single-sex communities than they did in coed communities. African Americans participated more in all-African American communities than they did in multiracial communities.

Working with innovative marketing services companies like Communispace, marketers are learning how to use social networking to better inform their market research efforts. In these small, gated digital communities, they can observe and participate in their customers' conversations. They engage participants with surveys, discussion threads, brainstorms, and chats on specific topics. This direct view into consumers' discussions reveals their needs, likes, and dislikes, and leads to a deeper marketing awareness that can be applied to product creation, concept testing, messaging development, and even shelf and packaging design.

Insights derived from these digital laboratories have already helped major marketers shape and strengthen their brand strategies. General Mills has learned much more about the buying, media, and brand preferences of Wal-Mart moms, a critical target segment. Insights regarding indulgence and portion control inspired Kraft to create 100-calorie packs of its consumers' favorite snacks. Schwab's marketers identified unmet needs, tested pricing, and prioritized new services for the high-net-worth consumer segment.

In the always-on world, we can expect marketers to further shift their research spending away from syndicated research, focus groups, and "stop-the-presses" annual studies to ongoing dialogues with consumers that are rooted in everyday experience. Listening and responding to the voice of the consumer in this way requires work on multiple fronts. It can mean more face-to-face visits to truck stops, offices, grocery stores, and customers' homes. It often means investing in ethnographic research. And it inevitably means more smart and scalable intelligence gathering through consumer-focused digital media. It also means that the insight captured from these interactions doesn't get filed away in the bottom drawer of a midlevel planner—instead, it directly influences the strategic direction set by the CMO and other marketing leaders.

"We don't do market research. We spend time with people," says Jean-Pierre Petit, who heads Nike's soccer business in Europe. "Our designers and product people go to soccer games, or to the inline skaters at Trocadero, to connect with the kids. You can learn a lot from just watching and talking to them."

A similar kind of consumer-centric focus helped Volkswagen and its ad agency, Crispin Porter + Bogusky, produce its powerful, against-the-grain advertising for the 2007 Jetta (Exhibit 2-8). This "safe happens" campaign combined television and digitally based ads to tout the automobile's safety features. It used a combination of violence and realism that was engineered to hit the elusive sweet spot of Generation Y, the 18- to 27-year-olds who currently represent one of the most desirable consumer segments for marketers.

One typical example: two young men, driving down the road, are debating their use of the word *like*. Just as one of them says, "Stuff happens; stuff doesn't 'like' happen," a car suddenly pulls out in front of them and they crash. The ad then shows them standing next to the car, unhurt. One says to the other, "Holy—," and the commercial ends.

The delicate balance of the dialogue could never have been struck without substantiation from the field that it would not just catch the attention of young drivers, but connect with them. These ads are not just edgy, but deeply informed by consumer insight, from the abrupt

attention-getting theatrics to the safety message to the realism of the dialogue.

The time is ripe to explore these new avenues to customer insight, because the methods for gathering and synthesizing such insight are still in their infancy. According
to research conducted on the marketing and media ecosystem by Booz Allen Hamilton in association with the Association of National Advertisers, the Internet Advertising Bureau, and the American Association of Advertising
Agencies, less than 25 percent of marketers believe that
they have the suite of capabilities in place today to make
them "digitally savvy" and therefore sufficiently equipped
to address the challenges of the always-on world.

At the same time, 80 percent of marketers acknowl-
edge that the importance of consumer insights has grown
dramatically in the last five years, and 60 percent of them

are moving to measure media usage behaviors regularly as part of their consumer insight efforts. As American Express CMO John Hayes says, "The world is in the middle of an ongoing conversation. Being in the conversation is worth a lot, because that's where you create relevance, that's where you create an affinity for your products, and that's how you start to sell."

THE CONSUMER'S NEW NATURE

New forms of customer insight will arrive just in time to meet the consumers of the twenty-first century: multiple generations of shoppers who, each day, become more difficult to understand, let alone to reach, through conventional marketing mechanisms. They are media-savvy to the point of being almost media-immune. At least four different generations, as defined by conventional demographic wisdom, are relevant in the always-on era, each with its own way of making life challenging for marketers, media companies, and agencies:

The Baby Boom Generation

The baby boom generation was born between the late 1940s and the early 1960s—the postwar years. This group, which is currently approaching retirement, has dominated marketing since its early years, largely because of its relatively large population in North America and Europe.

In the twenty-first-century consumer marketplace, the boomers are the analog generation—they grew up watching broadcast television and listening to vinyl record albums. But they were also the first generation to truly recognize the power of digital media en masse: Microsoft founder Bill Gates, Apple Computer founder Steve Jobs, and World Wide Web inventor Tim Berners-Lee are all members of this group (all were born in 1955, one year after its population peaked). Known for being idealistic (some would say preachy, others self-obsessed), this generation has a tradition of demanding the most from the institutions around it while resisting their domination.

One of the ironies of this generation is that the baby boom years ushered in a fixation on youth in media and advertising that has never quite disappeared. But that must change; the rising number of people over 50 alone will ensure that. Always voracious consumers who have been inventive in articulating their demands, the boomers are already calling for a vast array of products and services to help them navigate their golden years.

Generation X

Generation X, also known as "slackers," "generation bof," and the "baby bust" generation, was born between the assassination of U.S. President John F. Kennedy and the first years of President Ronald Reagan's term. *Bof*, a French word for "whatever," is fitting for this generation, whose cynical worldview was shaped by growing up in difficult economic times. This group is far smaller in numbers than the baby boomers; its formative years stretched from the 1970s oil crisis to the recession of the early 1990s.

Slackers were the earliest Atari enthusiasts and the first generation to fully immerse itself in video games. Cable television channels such as MTV and CNN shaped their attitudes. They grew up in front of the TV; the "latchkey children" of the 1970s are members of this generation. Yet they are not easily persuaded by any form of mass advertising. Slackers often want to build more solid families, but sometimes feel that they lack the emotional and financial wherewithal needed to do so. Many of them grew up with the expectation that they would not be able to live as well, or as easily, as their parents. Nor do they necessarily feel included in the increasingly prominent efforts to gain the attention of their younger counterparts in Generation Y.

Generation X was the first true PC generation—a heritage of hands-on technology that helps explain why its constituents are at the forefront of entrepreneurship and the Internet. Today, they're entering leadership positions throughout society, and in many instances, they are the principal drivers of the digital economy—think Jerry Yang of Yahoo!. Indeed, the "war for talent" in many industries is a reflection of the fact that this generation's numbers are smaller than those of the baby boom generation.

Gen X's skepticism and pragmatism have already begun to affect the prevailing culture in many countries, and they will do so even more strongly as its members come into their own. With Gen X in positions of influence, it will be very difficult for marketers to succeed with unsubstantiated or misleading claims.

Generation Y

The members of Generation Y, also known as the Millennials and the "echo boomers," are the children of the baby boomers—which means that their numbers are far greater than those of their Gen X predecessors. They include the more than 60 million U.S. consumers who were born between the launching of MTV in 1981 and the commercialization of the Internet in 1996; there are also about 90 million people this age in Europe and 20 million in Japan. The older members of this generation are just now moving into the mainstream adult arena of reliable cars and mortgages. Whereas Gen X spent a lot of time in front of the TV, Gen Y is the first generation that is always on. They're consumers of every imaginable means of communication: TV, radio, cell phone, Internet, video games—often simultaneously. They make no real distinction between cable and broadcast television because they've never known a world with less than triple-digit channel offerings. And by necessity they pay attention very selectively. Moreover, their early years were more optimistic than those of Generation X, a by-product of their boomer parents, who lavished both financial resources and emotional praise on them. They all think their content is important—whether it's video or text—and they crave interactivity, connection, and social validation. The popularity of social networks is in large part attributable to the Millennials' need to feel connected.

Each new generation requires more sophisticated advertising and media strategies, but Gen Y is particularly savvy. "They see through things right away," Cie Nicholson of PepsiCo cautions. "And they are more in control, especially when it comes to how they watch and consume media."

Although Gen Y may feel privileged and entitled, it is also a group that is coming of age in a time of political and economic insecurity. The simple truth is that, even with decades of experience communicating with young consumers, marketers may not know what they are in for with Generation Y. They are the first consumers whose habits have been shaped by digital media. They've been plugged in almost since birth—not just to the PC and the Web, but to mobile phones, social networks, instant messaging, and video games. They've been besieged with product messages in a media mix that's updated as quickly as technologies emerge. And they are fickle buyers. Instant communication, constant media use, and the demand for individualization have greatly constrained the life cycles of popular Gen Y brands and the campaigns that sell them.

Venkatesh Kini, Coca-Cola India's vice president of marketing, has had direct experience marketing Sprite to Generation Y, the soda's primary target market. After experimenting with several approaches, he found a winning message in this cheerfully cynical comment on the shallowness of celebrity endorsement: "Image is nothing. Obey your thirst." The key to Gen Y, suggests Kini, is the ability to deliver quickly on a demonstrably valuable promise. "Gen Y is growing up in an instant-gratification era, when music, news, and entertainment of any kind is available almost free, almost instantly, and in unlimited variety," he says. "That drives an extreme lack of patience with anything that doesn't appeal to that need for instant gratification."

Nor can marketers merely tweak traditional techniques, as they have in the past, to reach this group. Coming of age in the most brand-crazy period in history, Gen Ys expect a constant rush of new brands and new iterations of their favorite products; their tastes don't stay still very long. "By the time we recognize the wave, it's already crashing," adds Kini.

Gen Ys have already demonstrated how quickly their affinity for digital media can serve as a catalyst for entirely new categories of communication. For example, according to research from the National School Boards Association and Grunwald Associates LLC, 96 percent of U.S. students between the ages of 9 to 17 who are online have used social networking technology to connect with their peers. This is in a world where MySpace was founded in 2003 and Facebook in 2004.

In addition to migrating quickly to new media platforms such as social networks, Gen Y also has a reputation for moving easily across multiple platforms. As a result, marketing targeting this cohort must be increasingly interwoven so that an ad in one venue feeds off a different form of advertising in another. Thus, to promote their latest releases, film studios send trivia questions as text messages. Trailers, actor interviews, lost scenes, and other video previews are all part of a rich Web promotional mix.

Transforming a company's marketing philosophy to meet the needs of a demographic like Generation Y represents an extraordinary commitment, but it will pay off for decades to come. Marketers who attempt to understand Gen Ys now will have the jump on competitors as this group matures. After all, some of the biggest brands on the market today bonded with baby boomers early and rode with them from youth into middle age. The question is, will the brands that grew up with the boomers be able to reinvent themselves for Gen Y? Or will the big brands of the new millennium be names that most of us haven't even heard of yet?

Generation Z

Generation Z is today's children, born at the turn of the century and beyond. Currently below the age of 10, Gen Z

EXHIBIT 2-9 **TOTAL TIME SPENT WITH DIGITAL NOW EXCEEDING TELEVISION**

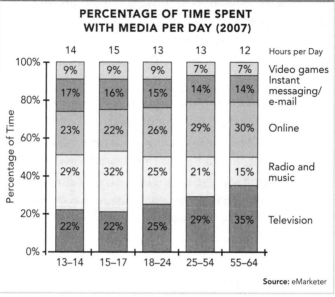

PERCENTAGE OF TIME SPENT WITH MEDIA PER DAY (2007)

Source: eMarketer

is growing up in a world that the rest of us created—one that is saturated with media and always on. How today's children—plugged in globally in record numbers—will react to their media environment as they mature will be a major demographic story for the next decade or more. Of one thing we can be sure: it is unwise to make predictions of a generation at a tender age.

As Exhibit 2-9 shows, the total amount of time that consumers spend with digital media now exceeds their couch time in front of the television. Interestingly, the media habits among generations are not as different as one might suspect. While Gen Y and Millennials drove the initial surge in new media, boomers are also spending significant amounts of time online. The younger generations are also spending more time listening to music, playing video games, and instant messaging.

Indeed, for marketers, there is still a great deal to learn about the behavior of each different consumer segment. Will each subsequent generation have its unique characteristics? Or does the shift to Gen X and Gen Y, at heart, represent a threshold movement toward a digitally focused society with fundamentally new rules for media, marketing, and retail? Stay tuned, as the networks used to tell us; our increasing sophistication in analyzing consumers in real time suggests that there will be much better ways to answer these questions in the not-so-distant future.

THE FIRST SIGNS OF CONSUMER CONTROL

Ultimately, today's marketing environment will be known in advertising history as the period when marketing practices caught up with reality—that is, when advertisers began to recognize that the consumer had the upper hand.

We're beginning to see evidence of this sea change in the way media dollars are apportioned. After a decade of continual increases in advertising budgets but relative stability in the channels in which advertising appears, many leading marketers are rebalancing their media mix. Specifically, they are directing more money and more attention to the Internet and other digital media. Newspapers and magazines are losing advertising to the Web; radio broadcasters are losing listeners, talent, and revenues to iPod playlists and satellite radio. Television networks also see the writing on the wall, as the penetration of broadband, game consoles, and next-generation set-top boxes heralds the rise of video on demand, video downloads, interactive game networks, Internet TV, and other broadcast- and cable-busting enterprises.

As marketers gain more experience with digital media and learn more about what resonates with their target consumers, they will further shape their advertising efforts with ever-increasing sophistication and precision. Thus, for example, Unilever has cashed in on the popularity of Evan and Garth, two characters it created to promote its Axe body spray, by expanding their presence from their Internet beginnings to video games, mobile devices, and television. In 2007, when Unilever unveiled a new Axe body spray scent, it took the opportunity to introduce its young men to its four comely new spokesmodels, the Bom Chicka Wah Wahs. And it did so with a digital experience housed on a Web site supported by ring tones, a faux "rockumentary" about the girl group, photos, viral elements to support blogging and other user-generated content, downloadable music, and even a real music video that was aired on MTV.

From where did this marketing spring? "We stay as close to the consumer as we can," says Kevin George, vice president, deodorants for Unilever U.S. "Three years ago we made the shift from 'behind the two-way mirror' to using ethnography to generate insights. Observing what consumers actually do—rather than what they say they do—has made a huge difference. Talking to them about things other than the product and brand offers a much deeper understanding of who they are and what motivates them."

Unilever's commitment to connecting consumer insight to advertising innovation appears to be paying off. Today Unilever commands an 80 percent share of the U.S. male body-spray market.

THIS BUD'S FOR DIGITAL

Some of the lessons of the future of advertising will not be learned easily. In 2007, Anheuser-Busch (AB) used the Super Bowl as a launching pad for Bud.tv, its ambitious digital entertainment destination. The reasoning was solid: AB's target audience of multitasking young men between the ages of 21 and 29 was leaving TV, with the exception of live sports, for video games, DVDs, iTunes, and the like. The value of the 30-second spot was in question, with new technologies and entertainment options proliferating. And there was a sense of urgency that AB needed to learn the new rules of digital media both fast and firsthand.

Bud.tv was indeed an aggressive response to these conditions. Its vision was to be a digital entertainment network, with comedy, music, and sports content controlled and programmed by AB. The creative elements would not be designed to focus exclusively on beer per se, but rather on the lifestyle of its target audience. Eventually, AB hoped to build up the Bud.tv audience to as many as two to three million unique visitors per month.

Yet, despite an initial investment of somewhere between $20 and $30 million, Bud.tv has not been the commercial success that AB anticipated. In fact, it managed to attract only 200,000 to 300,000 monthly unique visitors when it was launched in February 2007, and these numbers soon drifted downward to 150,000—a figure that in no way quenched Anheuser-Busch's digital thirst.

What happened? For one thing, the requirement that viewers be age-verified as 21 or over prevented many of the most interested would-be visitors from getting into Bud.tv. Through some trial and error, AB also learned that although its short-form digital content was compelling enough to connect directly with young men, the strategy aimed at driving them to the company's own destination site was not working.

To reach its consumers, the brewer needed to go where large numbers of young men already were—with edgy content that could be easily accessed and shared. That led AB to YouTube, where "Swear Jar," AB's risqué 60-second spot that was considered too hot for the 2007 Super Bowl, quickly achieved more than three million views.

Since then, AB has publicly, but somewhat less than wholeheartedly, committed itself to Bud.tv through at least the end of 2008. "I think [Bud.tv] is something that could have an ending someday," said Tony Ponturo, vice president of global media and sports/entertainment marketing, "but I think if we keep learning from it and if we keep seeing assets from it, then it makes sense to continue the site. . . .

> We have to keep evolving it. We need to work better on getting traffic and relatable content. We're also trying to find ways to create a dialogue with the consumer so there's a chance for chat and text. We need to build that platform out a little bit more."
> And Bud.tv will be far from AB's only ongoing online effort. In 2008, the company plans to spend some 10 to 15 percent of its estimated $500 million media budget online.

In addition to producing their own programming and designing their own Web environments, smart marketers will also recognize the demand for consumer control by finding ways to make advertising and programming more interactive. This means more than just click-the-remote capabilities or the ability to browse or search. "Consumers are telling us that they want to be in control of the storytelling," says Beth Comstock, president of integrated media at NBC Universal. "And, as a part of that desire, they want to engage in advertising in different ways. There will be times when the old kind of passive experience is going to be just right. But increasingly, consumers want to filter, they want to act, they want to be a part of the experience. And we have to be smart about it."

PepsiCo did just that in a campaign that began in late 2006. "We launched MDX, a carbonated soft drink with energy credentials," explains Cie Nicholson of Pepsi North America. "To support it, we used a 'Stay Sharp' campaign that quizzed consumers on their alertness. We showed them a user-generated video taken from YouTube, and then afterward we asked them a question about what they just saw. In one very cool spot, a guy is sitting there while everything changes around him. He's happy, he's sad, he's eating a pizza, he's drinking. At the end, the advertisement asks: 'How many pieces of pizza did he eat?' And you have no idea, but you can go on the Internet to find out. In another spot, we show two Claymation figures dancing, and one is a policeman. At the end, we ask how many prongs he had on his badge. Again, this is user-generated content. We're using video that people have put online. We decide what we'll use, so we're turning over creative control in a way that makes us comfortable."

Pepsi's experience contradicts the conventional marketing wisdom. It is striking how consistently marketers have denigrated the idea that consumers want more interaction with their information and entertainment environment, and that they will pay more for the privilege. This skepticism dates back to the mid-1990s, when several high-profile interactive television experiments, ranging from Time Warner's Full Service Network to Microsoft's WebTV, essentially failed. Chastened digital revolutionaries returned to a view of television vaguely derived from Marshall McLuhan's assessment of it as a "cold" medium for "passive viewers" who preferred the "least objectionable programming" (that last phrase was coined by NBC programmer Paul Klein in the 1970s). Television, many believed, would remain forever distinct, in design, use, and location, from the computer.

But more recent media experiences suggest that the idea of viewer passivity is a myth. Interactive elements in TV shows from *Dancing with the Stars* to *Monday Night Football* are driving changes in consumers' usage patterns.

In an increasing number of living rooms and dens, the home PC sits right next to the TV, with both of them connected by broadband. According to the marketing research company BIGresearch, almost 7 in 10 online users reported watching TV while they are online. This phenomenon is, of course, a double-edged sword for media companies and their advertisers—it makes consumers a moving, potentially elusive target, but it also opens the way for a creative, compelling interplay between TV and online media.

In fact, the television-to-Web connection may become the biggest source of added value for TV advertising. Pontiac's campaign for the 2006 Solstice provided a powerful illustration of that potential. An episode of Donald Trump's reality show *The Apprentice* challenged teams to develop a brochure to support the roadster's launch. During the episode, NBC ran a 60-second spot advertising the Solstice, encouraging interested viewers to learn more at a program-specific Web site and to register to preorder an exclusive version of the new car. Within just 15 minutes after the spot aired, traffic to the site grew by some 1,400 percent. Moreover, searches for "Pontiac Solstice" and "Pontiac" increased 190 and 369 percent, respectively, during the week the *Apprentice*/Solstice episode aired. Not only did Pontiac sell 1,000 of the special version of the Solstice, but this TV-to-Web connection generated thousands of additional buyers for its regular production models.

The dramatic growth of user-generated media is another strong argument against consumer passivity. As the cost of crafting and distributing creative content continues to decline, adults and children alike are jumping into the production game, fashioning playlists, online period-

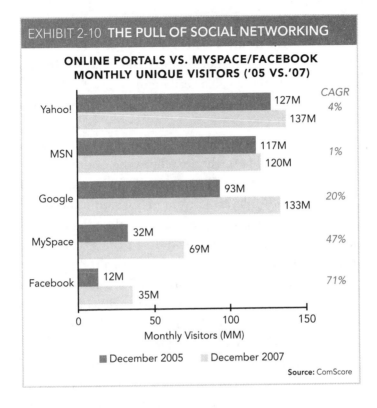

EXHIBIT 2-10 **THE PULL OF SOCIAL NETWORKING**

**ONLINE PORTALS VS. MYSPACE/FACEBOOK
MONTHLY UNIQUE VISITORS ('05 VS.'07)**

Yahoo! — 127M / 137M — CAGR 4%
MSN — 117M / 120M — 1%
Google — 93M / 133M — 20%
MySpace — 32M / 69M — 47%
Facebook — 12M / 35M — 71%

Monthly Visitors (MM)

■ December 2005   ▨ December 2007

Source: ComScore

icals, original music recordings and films, and elaborately personalized Web sites. Today, about 12 million Americans maintain their own blogs. In January 2008, Facebook, the self-proclaimed "social utility that connects you with the people around you," reported that it had more than 61 million active users and had been adding an average of 250,000 new registrations per day since January 2007. In just two years, the social networking site MySpace more than doubled, while online portals grew incrementally (see Exhibit 2-10). The shopping site eBay—a consumer-created destination where the content is a seemingly infinite variety of sales information—has roughly 79 million unique consumers visiting its marketplaces each month. Finally, ComScore data from November 2007 suggest that Google's YouTube has 74.5 million visitors and is streaming 2.9 billion on-demand videos each month or 39 videos per visitor—many of which are produced by consumers, not professionals.

The expanding popularity of online multiplayer games and virtual worlds further explodes the notion of consumer passivity. In the fantasy game "World of Warcraft," founded in 1994, players join one of two battling hordes in a world of humans, orcs, elves, and dwarfs with highly realistic visuals and rigorously defined rules that govern each character's ability to communicate, gain skills, fight, purchase supplies, and learn. By July 2007, its subscriber base had reached 9 million people worldwide. Second Life, a virtual world launched in 2003, is famous for having its own currency and community-like structure, and while there are no reliable statistics on active use, there were more than 8 million membership accounts active in 2007. Habbo, an eight-year-old virtual world created by the Finnish company Sulake, reported some 76 million avatars in 22 countries in 2007.

These virtual worlds, which combine elements of social networking and video games, are already demonstrating how new forms of consumer behavior will have a real-world impact on the future of advertising and marketing. Blue-chip marketers, including PepsiCo, Starwood, Toyota, Adidas, IBM, Coca-Cola, Dell, and Sun Microsystems, are experimenting actively in this emerging medium. For example, they are building dealerships, hotels, and other services in Second Life. By doing so, they are following some of their prime marketing targets—the key influencers and early adopters who have migrated to these cutting-edge offerings. But perhaps more importantly, they are preparing for the time when tomorrow's consumers may move there as well. In 2007, *e-marketer* reported that 24 percent of the 34.3 million U.S. Internet users between the ages of 3 and 17 would visit virtual worlds once a month. And it predicts that by 2010 the usage figure will double to close to 50 percent.

Do virtual engagements lead to offline results? If a consumer tricks out a Scion in the virtual world, will he or she end up in a real-world showroom? At this point, no one really knows. But the promise of deep, unfiltered consumer insight is already an intriguing promise of the virtual-world future. Habbo, for example, has already discovered that the online usage of its predominantly teenage user base can be transformed into a wealth of data and insight related to this audience's interests—specifically, the brands these people like, how they spend their time and money, and what they recommend to their friends. With that resource in hand, Habbo is now actively surveying its users and selling what it learns to interested corporations.

The rise of customer-centrism has raised concerns about privacy in the past, and it will raise more concerns about it in the future. Conceivably, Generation Z will react against being "data mined" enough to make marketers take notice; more likely, new methods of tracking customer interest and behavior will be so commonplace within a few years that no one will notice them. The most visible result will be relevance: the greater the in-depth understanding of consumers that marketers have, the more meaningful and relevant their advertising will be.

And so far, at least, people seem interested in having

advertising be more relevant to them. As many as 55 percent of the respondents in one Yankelovich study said that they would pay extra to receive more personalized marketing. Other studies confirm that the Internet is an increasingly important medium for prepurchase information—particularly in categories like health care and automobiles, for which consumers used to obtain information primarily from one-way media like magazines. These days, it may be that a contextually relevant and targeted ad online may have more impact than a flashy article in a magazine or a slick TV spot.

Whatever the medium, always-on consumers cannot be bullied, conquered, or treated like commodities. They must be engaged by clarity, and marketers, media companies, and ad agencies need to develop the ability to discover exactly what turns them on and what turns them off. In this environment where the consumer is in control, the only way to reach people is to create an indisputable link between a brand's distinctive attributes and consumers' lives. And in a way, that's the lightning in a bottle that has made for great marketing since the dawn of modern advertising.

There may come a time when each major company has its own customer-review site, in which consumers let one another know about the particular product or service that is most applicable to them. If that happens, brand loyalty will not just be a matter of consumers continuing to purchase the product or recommending it to others, but rather of consumers finding it easy to contribute to the company's advertising and to use that contribution as a form of self-expression. Like Microsoft, which depends on volunteer aficionados in its online technical support message boards, more and more companies will rely on their "prosumers" or "brand advocates" to help other consumers navigate among the complexities of their offerings. If not enough consumers are willing to do so, that in itself will be seen as a condemnation of the quality of the company's products.

But benefiting from direct consumer participation will be the ultimate payoff from a commitment to a customer-centric marketing focus. And ultimately that consumer participation will be an integral part of the marketing efforts of every company that works hard, works smart, and plays to win. Indeed, a consumer-driven focus will influence just about everything that happens in successful companies—research, product development, supply-chain management, sales, and, ultimately, advertising.

Especially now that your consumers are always on.

RESOURCES

- *CMO Thought Leaders: The Rise of the Strategic Marketer.* strategy+business Books, 2007, http://www.strategy-business.com.

- Landry, Ed, Chris Vollmer, and Carolyn Ude, "HD Marketing 210: Sharpening the Conversation," Booz Allen Hamilton, October 2007.

- "How Marketers Hone Their Aim Online," *Wall Street Journal*, July 19, 2007.

- National School Boards Association (NSBA) and Grunwald Associates LLC, *Creating and Connecting: Research and Guidelines on Online Social and Educational Networking*," August 2007.

- Foehr, Ulla G., *Media Multitasking among American Youth: Prevalence, Predictors and Pairings*, Kaiser Foundation, December 2006.

- For more resources and up-to-date information, see www.businessfuture.com.

3

MUTINY IN MEDIA

IT WAS MAY 2002, just before a breakfast seminar for media and marketing leaders at the Paley Center for Media (which was then known as the Museum of Television and Radio). Based in New York, this institution is devoted to the history of broadcasting—and history was weighing heavily on attendees' minds, or so it seemed from the chatter of arriving guests.

The major U.S. television broadcast networks were about to open their "upfront market," the concentrated period when they negotiate prices and sell the bulk of their advertising space for the fall season. Although the networks had experienced two decades of eroding viewership, prices for this inventory had risen almost unabated and yet another increase was imminent. A small group of executives and consultants in a corner of the room wondered how this could be.

"Ask *him*," said one member of the group, pointing to "Mr. X," the chief executive of a major television company, who had just sidled up and was listening with some amusement to the conversation. "It's the simple law of supply and demand," Mr. X answered. "Major marketers need to reach mass audiences, and we are the only game in town. They have the demand. We have the supply. And as with any product, as that supply gets harder to find, you can charge more for it."

Mr. X's complacency was understandable. In his world, media distribution was constrained. The programmer/editor was in control, and marketers had few alternatives to the prime-time TV show, the four-color magazine ad, or the newspaper insertion for reaching mass audiences. Every year the pundits predicted dramatic change: the convergence of analog and digital media, the erosion of mass audiences, and the restructuring of the media and advertising industries. Yet every year, leading industry practices remained static, even stagnant, and the overall pattern of marketing spending barely budged.

Nevertheless, Mr. X's complacency was about to be shattered. For in just a few years in the mid-2000s, the competing platforms in media have exploded, irrevocably changing the ways in which consumers absorb entertainment and information—and how they perceive and engage with brands. In turn, marketers have fundamentally altered their views about where and how to connect with consumers and have further reshaped the media environment.

Consider the following:

➤ Volvo launched its S60 sedan with a $10 million campaign conducted exclusively online.

➤ Absolut Vodka and Ford each spend 20 percent of their total marketing dollars online.

- GM Certified's used-vehicles division is allocating 85 percent of its advertising budget to online media.

- Microsoft says that the majority of its $1 billion annual advertising budget will "shift to digital" by 2010.

- Pfizer is partnering with Sermo, an online social network of licensed physicians, in order to talk directly to the site's 31,000 members.

- Advertising.com, an advertising network comprising thousands of Web sites, reaches more online sports fans each month than major destination brands, such as ESPN and Fox Sports.

And what of Mr. X, who once seemed so confident about running the only game in town? He lost his job a couple of years later and now, ironically, is the head of a digital media company.

CONSUMER ATTENTION SPLITS

The upheaval in media is more profound than any series of bullet points—or job changes—might suggest. Audiences for many traditional media continue to stagnate and, in many cases, are in decline. Digital media platforms, such as broadband, video game consoles, and mobile devices, are reaching critical mass and attracting large, loyal audiences of their own (see Exhibit 3-1). Consumers, media execs, and marketers are confronted with an ever-expanding mix of media and entertainment options.

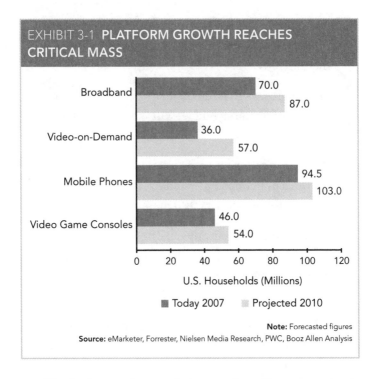

EXHIBIT 3-1 PLATFORM GROWTH REACHES CRITICAL MASS

Broadband: 70.0 / 87.0
Video-on-Demand: 36.0 / 57.0
Mobile Phones: 94.5 / 103.0
Video Game Consoles: 46.0 / 54.0

U.S. Households (Millions)

■ Today 2007　■ Projected 2010

Note: Forecasted figures
Source: eMarketer, Forrester, Nielsen Media Research, PWC, Booz Allen Analysis

The bad news for marketers and media companies is that because consumers are no longer concentrated in just a few media sectors, they are more difficult to find. The good news: many new media platforms are highly interactive, creating the opportunity for two-way exchanges that have the potential for greater targeting, relevance, and engagement.

More media options have naturally led to audience fragmentation. In 1985, the average U.S. household received 19 television channels. Ten years later, that number had more than doubled, to 41. By 2005, the figure had risen to 96. The impact on audiences was highlighted in a recent study of British television. It found that in 1999, 153 shows boasted audiences of 15 million viewers or more. By

2004, the number was only four. In 2007, there was no U.K. program with an audience that large. The challenge of fragmentation is just as dramatic online. From 2000 to 2006, the number of Web sites increased from about 16 million to 62 million—with a large part of the recent growth being driven by sites with one million or fewer unique visitors each month. The major portals, including Yahoo!, MSN, and Google, do capture about 60 percent of all online advertising, but they capture only about 25 percent of all consumer page views. In fact, today nearly 50 percent of all online traffic is registered on sites with relatively small audiences: one million or fewer visitors each month.

This fragmentation of online audiences has spawned new competitors to the major portals and media companies. These competitors are advertising networks. Representing myriad smaller sites, they aggregate ad-placement opportunities and sell them to advertisers. Many smaller sites sell their entire ad inventory through these networks, and most large publishers use them to sell remnant inventory. Some of these ad networks have corralled enormous audiences in this way: ValueClick, Tribal Fusion, Specific Media, Casale Media Network, and Traffic Marketplace are all ranked in the top 20 largest Web properties, with more than 100 million unique visitors per month.

The success of advertising networks is driven at least in part by the fact that marketers need both large *and* targeted audiences. The ad networks make it easier for marketers to buy and place their advertising where the consumers are predisposed to want it. And marketers benefit from the efficiency inherent in buying space on many sites at once at volume prices. The smaller sites and publishers benefit economically too; ad networks give them scale through packaging that they could never achieve on their own. And as ad networks improve their audience-targeting capabilities, it is highly likely that their share of online advertising will continue to grow. This is a major reason why successful companies in this space, including Advertising.com, Tacoda, Blue Lithium, aQuantive (DrivePM), and 24/7 Real Media, have been acquired by the likes of AOL, Yahoo!, Microsoft, and WPP.

PRIME TIME ON AISLE THREE

The explosion in media options is not restricted to traditional and digital platforms. It has spread to the point of purchase in retailing, too.

The point of purchase is extremely valuable advertising territory. Almost 70 percent of consumer purchase decisions are made at the shelf—with 53 percent of those purchases made on impulse. In addition, marketers increasingly view the store environment as a place to reinforce advertising messages communicated through other media. Furthermore, the retail environment remains comparatively uncluttered with advertising, providing marketers with the opportunity to deliver messages without the diffusion of attention that is inevitable with television, print, and online media consumed at home.

The result: a boom in shopper marketing—typically defined as in-store media, consumer and trade promotion, product sampling, and custom displays, targeted at the consumer selecting a product from a shelf. According to a study by the Grocery Manufacturers Association and

Deloitte and Touche, shopper marketing is expected to grow at a rate of 21 percent annually through 2010. In other words, it ranks only behind the Internet as the fastest-growing advertising platform for marketers.

Media companies have always longed to find opportunities to gain a share of this "below-the-line" marketing spending. And with traditional spending expanding in single digits overall, some media companies are finding shopper marketing—especially in-store media, which drives video-based advertising to the point of purchase—a tempting entry point.

TRADITIONALLY, marketing spending has been split into *above-the-line* and *below-the-line* components. Above-the-line spending refers to the costs associated with advertising in conventional measured media, such as newspapers, magazines, radio, and television. Below-the-line spending refers to all other media and promotion activity, including consumer and trade promotions, word-of-mouth marketing, direct marketing, PR, sponsorships, company Web sites, event marketing, and shopper aisle marketing.

In-store media could well invigorate the retail shopping environment. The use of even the most basic kinds of in-store television advertising delivers estimated sales lifts ranging from 15 to 60 percent, depending on the store, the season, and the item. And as in-store media programming and measurement become more sophisticated, their importance in the media and marketing mix, like that of ad networks, is likely to increase significantly.

Of course, this medium is still regarded as experimental. It competes for only a small fraction of marketers' available spending, and it has no permanent year-to-year place in most of their budgets. In fact, advertisers spend only about $330 million annually on in-store media networks—a very modest figure compared to the $75 billion spent on broadcast and cable advertising. The lack of reliable metrics has also slowed down adoption rates. Finally, its video content, in terms of production values and creative, doesn't yet equal the potential of the medium.

Nevertheless, the common-sense appeal of in-store media is strong enough that the question of its maturation begins with *when*, not *if*. The major researchers, including Nielsen, TNS, and Arbitron, have invested in developing new metrics in support of in-store media analytics. And major media companies, such as CBS (via its Sign-Storey acquisition) and NBC Universal (with its PRN advertising sales partnership), have already positioned themselves to participate in the new platform. Given the improved metrics, more compelling programming, and advertising sales innovation that these players will bring, it is a safe bet that marketer spending on in-store media will grow. The strongest indicator of future growth is perhaps the growing interest in in-store media in the consumer goods sector. A 2007 Booz Allen survey with Demand Tec and the Trade Promotion Management Association highlighted that 46 percent of consumer goods companies plan to increase their investment in in-store media over the next two years.

IN-STORE MEDIA: COMING TO A SHELF NEAR YOU

The potential of in-store media is best demonstrated by the industry's largest player, Premier Retail Networks (PRN). PRN, a San Francisco–based division of Thomson Multimedia, boasts screens in more than 6,000 stores and operates Wal-Mart TV, the nation's largest in-store media network. With more than 125,000 screens in some 3,150 stores, Wal-Mart itself offers advertisers a potential audience of 130 million shoppers every four weeks. PRN also serves Costco, Sam's Club, Best Buy, and Circuit City.

Although PRN is the biggest in-store media operator, other companies have also built significant networks. Target has Channel Red, the first retailer-owned in-store network, which spans its chain. In 2007, CBS acquired SignStorey, a provider of in-store media networks for grocery retailers that operates in 1,300 chains and has clients that include Super Value, Pathmark, ShopRite, and Price Chopper. CBS has since rebranded the company as CBS Outernet.

While the list of in-store media players continues to grow, Bentonville's giant retailer has been in the closed-network business for 10 years, longer than anyone else. A decade ago, the programming in Wal-Mart stores was a single loop playing the same shows throughout each store. Because no one quite knew how to use video in the retail environment, the screens were placed high above the aisles—close enough to be intrusive but far enough away so that the information being delivered never quite merged with the shopping experience.

Today, satellite-driven broadcast technology allows Wal-Mart to deliver different messages to different departments. And soon, new Internet-based distribution will allow the retailer to deploy different programming to individual screens within departments. There have been other refinements, too. The sound volume, for instance, is automatically adjusted to reflect shopper traffic patterns.

PRN's flat panel monitors now serve up paid advertising, as well as news, weather, and entertainment segments. Shoppers might see a video infomercial sponsored by Listerine or a demonstration of how the Agent CoolBlue prebrushing rinse turns plaque blue. They also might view Wal-Mart workers, sponsored by Dove soap, talking about health and well-being and programming from Nickelodeon's "Kids' Choice Awards" that has been repurposed for viewing in the children's aisles—along with supporting merchandising messages.

ADVERTISING SPENDING SHIFTS

When the history of early twenty-first-century marketing is written, it likely will be seen as a time when the marketing mix caught up with consumer behavior. After a decade of regular increases in marketing budgets but relative stability in media choices, many leading marketers—Anheuser-Busch, Procter & Gamble, and Johnson & Johnson, to name a few—have reappraised their assortment of communication channels. These companies are directing more money and attention to digital media and to a wide variety of below-the-line media services and offerings, such as shopper marketing, public relations, direct marketing, and event marketing.

The growth rates in marketing spending make this shift very clear. Between 2004 and 2006, above-the-line spending in traditional media grew by 1.7 percent annually. By contrast, in that same period, "below-the-line" spending grew by 6 percent annually, and Internet advertising grew by 26.5 percent.

The shift in marketers' advertising priorities is also visible in media company revenues. According to an analysis across 19 major media companies published by the *Silicon Valley Insider*, advertising revenues from the second quarter of 2006 to the same period in 2007 at the largest digital companies—specifically Google, Microsoft, Yahoo!, and AOL—grew by $866 million, or 26 percent. In comparison, newspapers and magazines declined by $170 million, or 5 percent; radio shrank by $90 million, or 5 percent; and television (a blend of both broadcast and cable) managed to increase by $220 million, or 3 percent, almost entirely on the backs of high single digit cable network performance. In an environment characterized by many traditional media losing share to digital, only outdoor, with its distinct out-of-home positioning, achieved a healthy double-digit increase, growing by 13 percent.

This fundamental shift in spending is just beginning. Look at the current mismatch in advertising spending within the automobile industry. Today, carmakers spend 50 percent of their marketing dollars on television and only about 4 to 5 percent online. But television advertising has a 27 percent impact on the consumer's decision to purchase a car, while more than 20 percent of the purchase decision is driven by online. The implication for carmakers: less ad spending on television and more spending online.

As the new generation of media-savvy CMOs emphasizes advertising accountability as well as media innovation, it is certain that their marketing mixes will catch up to the consumer. In part, this shift represents advertisers' growing displeasure with traditional media, most particularly broadcast television, which has continued to raise advertising prices while its efficacy as a conduit to consumers has declined. It also reflects the increasingly strong financial returns that marketers are getting on their digital investments. We have reached the stage where enough consumers are spending enough time accessing entertainment and information through enough new-

BELOW THE LINE: LIVE IN CENTRAL PARK

The track record of below-the-line media for successfully introducing new brands and profitably building sales has made it increasingly appealing to marketers. Witness the event marketing that American Express used to launch its credit card, Blue, in 1999:

"We hosted a Sheryl Crow concert in Central Park. In fact, we created and produced the event, which was very different from buying something off the shelf—a network spot, for instance," recalls CMO John Hayes. "We 'owned' the city of New York for the two weeks leading up to it. We wanted it broadcast live and Fox picked it up. The whole program cost less than a commercial in the Super Bowl, but it was much more valuable. . . . Through this event, we signaled to the market that this was a different product with a different personality."

The bottom line, according to Hayes: "Great launch momentum. Great level of understanding. Good positioning."

media platforms—beginning with cable and now including Web sites, video game consoles, iPods, PlayStations, and mobile phones—to transform the overall pattern of media usage.

These trends—audience fragmentation, the rise of competing solutions for dealing with it (such as ad networks, in-store media, and event marketing), and the ongoing shift in advertising spending—add up to an urgent case for change for media companies. To ensure that they are on the growth side of these developments, media companies need to

> Adopt the new mindset of the marketer: dialogue, accountability, relevance.

> Put the consumer at the center of their programming, marketing, audience research, and advertising sales efforts.

➤ Make their advertising inventory more interactive and offer new forms of ad customization and targeting.

➤ Develop integrated solutions that include an ever-greater diversity of marketing channels. (For traditional media companies, this will require a substantial expansion of their digital ventures and capabilities, and connecting their media and skills to below-the-line offerings.)

Underlying all these new practices is one fundamental skill. You could call it the skill of "media reinvention." It is the capability that at the end of the day will give some media companies the ability to help marketers make the best advertising and marketing choices in an era of unprecedented complexity. The mandate for media reinvention is clear, and media companies will be developing effective strategies to connect with dozens, if not hundreds, of differentiated audiences—in compelling ways that create demonstrable value for advertisers.

MEDIA REINVENTION IN A POST-ANALOG WORLD

Some traditional media companies have already recognized the post-analog, always-on mandate. They are acting in two ways, often simultaneously. They are working hard to increase the value of their existing media platforms through new strategies and technologies, and they are investing to achieve sizable positions across a wide range of new channels, including online video, social networking such as blogs and chat rooms, digital content environments, video gaming, in-store media, mobile devices, relationship marketing, and even e-commerce. Here are a few examples.

ESPN's Ad Sales Force Goes Consumer-Centric

ESPN's ad sales representatives used to work within media silos; a rep in the company's cable networks business didn't sell magazine ads or sponsorships. Now they are encouraged to create advertising solutions that follow targeted audiences across multiple media platforms in the quest for greater impact and, of course, larger deals.

"If we're surrounding consumers with media, we're going to give advertisers the opportunity to do the same thing," explained John Skipper, then head of ESPN's nontelevision operations, including ESPN.com and *ESPN the Magazine*, and head of ad sales for all of ESPN and ABC Sports. In response to this desire, ESPN reorganized its advertising sales function to emphasize an "agnostic" multiplatform approach, where focus is aligned with how consumers connect with the company's various media brands. When calling on marketers and agencies now, ESPN ad sales professionals arrive with portfolios that include cable, magazine, radio, online, mobile, video games, and sponsorship opportunities.

Multiplatform sales are complex, often custom-made, and require significant internal collaboration. One substantial barrier is finding salespeople who can think both creatively and horizontally across media to solve client problems. But multiplatform selling is working at ESPN.

For instance, in September 2007, GMC launched "Keys to Victory," a 16-week campaign mirroring the NFL season and its largest advertising effort ever. The campaign used ESPN inventory drawn from *Monday Night Football*, *ESPN the Magazine*, ESPN.com, and mobile to tap into GMC's target consumers' love of football.

These types of sales can be very rewarding; indeed, they are critical to serving the needs of larger marketers. In 2005, about 50 percent of ESPN's deals in excess of $2 million were multiplatform. In 2007, Ed Erhardt, president of ESPN customer marketing and sales, indicated that this percentage would increase to 75 percent and that ESPN would sign an additional 50 to 60 multiplatform deals—a record for the company.

AN OCTOBER 2007 STUDY by Booz Allen Hamilton and the Association of National Advertisers discovered that marketers are leaning toward media companies for assistance in the always-on world. When asked which of their partners—media companies, media buyers, communications planning agencies, or traditional full-service agencies—will become more important to them in the future, 52 percent of marketers cited media companies, while only 26 percent cited traditional full-service agencies.

Time Warner's Big-Idea Department

Time Warner's Global Media Group has taken on the job of building creative-driven, multiplatform initiatives for the media conglomerate's top 50 advertisers. Its goal: to discover how to add value for these major advertisers above and beyond what Time Warner's individual divisions can create on their own. To create and develop big ideas, Time Warner recognized that it needed a new and different kind of talent. It hired two former Young & Rubicam advertising agency executives—John Partilla as the group's president, and Mark D'Arcy as chief creative officer—to build a team with both creative and media strategy expertise. The group also works in tandem with external agencies.

Home Depot's "Home Show '06" campaign is a good example of one of Global Media's big ideas. When the world's largest home improvement retailer wanted to attract more consumers to its retail stores and Web site, the group combined live demonstrations and celebrity clinics in over 1,000 of the chain's stores with the construction of a "virtual house" online. Global Media reached across Time Warner to execute the idea, pulling together both media and editorial content from three different businesses—AOL's online platform, Time Inc.'s magazines, and the Turner Broadcasting System's cable networks.

Vogue's In-House Agency

With the 2004 founding of Vogue Studio, Condé Nast's *Vogue* magazine expanded into the agency business. Vogue Studio is an in-house agency that is based on the premise that no outside agency can deliver creative more attuned to *Vogue's* audience than *Vogue* itself.

The Studio has enabled *Vogue* to move upstream, beyond its clients' transactional media buying processes, to influence more strategic media and marketing decision making. Once the *Vogue* ad sales department identifies clients that could benefit from a more consultative approach, the Studio creates and pitches ad solutions that involve all of *Vogue* magazine's various platforms—print, events, online video, Internet, and mobile. The ability to deliver agency services has helped *Vogue* attract and expand relationships with a diverse and profitable group of clients, including Bergdorf Goodman, Cartier, Tourneau, Samsung, and even Wal-Mart.

Wal-Mart employed Vogue Studio to convince women to mix and match its clothing and accessories with high-priced designer labels to create stylish and cost-conscious outfits. Naturally, the two-year campaign, which was kicked off with an eight-page spread in September 2005, ran in the pages of *Vogue*. It also garnered 37 million press impressions, including stories in the *Wall Street Journal*, *BusinessWeek*, *USA Today*, and the *Los Angeles Times*.

MTV Brands the Virtual World

It may seem as if all the most powerful media innovations of recent years have come from outside the industry (think Google, YouTube, MySpace, and even craigslist), but then there's Viacom's MTV Networks. MTVN, which pioneered the music video revolution a quarter-century ago, has steadily and quietly been giving ventures such as Second Life a run for their money in the rapidly expanding space in the media world occupied by virtual worlds.

MTVN has been morphing its cable brands into virtual digital environments and, in the process, is creating high-engagement platforms for young people and the advertisers that want to connect with them. According to MTVN, its Virtual Laguna Beach draws users to the site 1.4 times per week, with each visit lasting an average of 37 minutes. By the end of 2007, MTVN was operating nine of these "worlds" and had a tenth milieu, Virtual Lower East Side, in development. And although Second Life gets great press for its roughly 9 million registered users, approximately 70 percent of whom are outside the United States and less than a million are active monthly inhabitants, far fewer observers are aware that MTVN has amassed 5.5 million registered users across Nicktropolis and its MTV-based virtual worlds as well as 3 to 4 million active monthly visitors to Neopets.

What's in it for advertisers? According to MTVN's metrics, 99 percent of the consumers who enter their virtual worlds are exposed to branded content, and 85 percent voluntarily interact with branded content.

Scripps Gets Direct with Consumers

The E.W. Scripps Company may have been founded on print, but it has a history of adopting emerging media platforms in profitable ways. It owns broadcast and cable television networks, newspapers, and interactive media. Today, it is driving hard to use these assets to create more direct consumer relationships.

Scripps is notable for its use of database marketing to develop deep insight into the interests and behaviors of its audiences. It has accomplished this mainly through digital means, such as online contests, branded opt-in e-newsletters, and online marketplaces.

The largest and most successful of these initiatives is the annual "HGTV Dream Home Giveaway." In 2006, the contest generated 6 million unique consumer registrations and 39 million individual entries. It also attracted sponsors and advertisers from across the marketing spectrum, including GMC, Lending Tree, and Lumber Liquidators.

Direct marketing venues, such as the Dream Home Giveaway, drive consumers to Scripps-branded registration Web sites, on which they provide information about themselves and their interests. These insights create a feedback loop that provides multiple opportunities for producing revenue: sponsored e-newsletters; marketplaces that connect consumers directly with relevant merchants; and behavioral insight that Scripps uses to improve the effectiveness of its online content, advertising, and on-air programming.

NBC Universal and News Corp.'s Hulu

Television's audiences may be declining, but the growth of online video proves that its content continues to exert a powerful pull on consumers and marketers. Consumers are watching more video content online—more than 40 percent watch at least one video per week. The majority of these consumers also appears to be accepting an ad-supported video business model. More than 50 percent are actually taking action after viewing a video advertisement. And most promising for the traditional media players, consumers appear to be more responsive to advertising in branded environments than in portals or sites featuring user-generated content. That's all good news for TV-focused players like NBC and Fox, which so far command a small share of the overall online video market.

These market dynamics are driving NBC Universal and Fox to create Hulu.com, an advertising-supported online video joint venture featuring television shows, short clips, and films that launched in beta in November 2007. The two companies see an opportunity to create a video offering around premium content that will attract both consumers' time and brand marketers' online spending. The importance of creating significant operational scale online has further compelled these two offline rivals to not only join together but also forge additional content deals with Sony and MGM.

Hulu.com is intended to be both an online consumer's "go-to" destination for high-quality video and a leading syndicator for other sites. "At the end of the day, we believe premium professional content wins," George Kliavkoff, NBC Universal's chief digital officer, told BusinessWeek.com. "We believe there is power in aggregating that content, and we believe in ubiquitous distribution."

To date, traditional media companies have used online video primarily to drive viewers to their own sites. But Hulu.com has entered into distribution agreements with MSN, Yahoo!, AOL, MySpace, and Comcast to ensure that its content has the broadest possible reach online. It is also encouraging consumers to embed its videos in their own sites as well as share them via e-mail. As both a destination and an "ad network," Hulu hopes to combine the high-engagement aspect of video, plus online's tracking and targeting capabilities, to further accelerate the shift of brand marketers to digital media.

The one thing that all of the above examples have in common is their focus on consumer insight and relevance. No matter what their strategic positioning, winning media companies will have to deliver both in full measure to attract consumers and marketers in the always-on world.

Toward this end, smart media companies are shifting their focus from *analyzing* their viewers to *knowing* them. They know that today's marketers want to know about consumer habits, preferences, and passions. When and how often do their target consumers visit Wal-Mart? Are they thinking about buying a new house or a car? How likely are they to tell a friend about a hot new brand or product? Marketers now expect media companies to help provide answers to these questions.

Thus, when the executives at NBC Universal describe the average viewer of the Bravo channel, the fact that the viewer is most likely an affluent woman aged 18–49 is only a starting point. More important, they know her interests: that she is an early adopter of fashion and consumer electronics and that she's an "affluencer"—affluent, engaged, and influential.

The data-rich media environment of digital companies gives them some advantages in the consumer insight

We need to have insights about how people consume media. If you're a big advertiser, you need to know about your consumer. But you depend on us to know how different audience segments consume their media
—Beth Comstock, president,
Integrated Media, NBC Universal.

and relevance game, but that does not mean that they can rest on their laurels. To demonstrate how well their digital offerings work as advertising platforms in concert with the other elements of a more diverse marketing mix, these organizations and their advertising sales teams must also find new opportunities to engage marketers and agencies with insights that show why their offerings drive better results.

For instance, Yahoo!'s dominance in online display ad sales is the result of a concentrated effort to become the Fortune 500's first choice in that realm. Toward this end, it has long emphasized cooperation between Silicon Valley and Madison Avenue and has invested in research designed to show how online advertising fits into everyday family life, the role the Internet plays in consumer decision making, and how young people around the world are using digital technology. In short, Yahoo! has broken out from the typical transactional sales pitch and has recognized the need to connect with marketers on a more strategic level.

For marketers who want to know the impact of their advertising, the best metric is sales. In 2003, Yahoo! partnered with Nielsen to develop an analytic platform designed to demonstrate the impact of online campaigns on sales growth. The "Consumer Direct" effort studied the habits of 20,000 households assembled from Nielsen's Homescan panel, correlating their exposure to online advertising with their purchase behavior. In 2007, Yahoo! partnered with comScore on a "Research Online, Buy Offline" study that measured the influence of paid search and display advertising as well as integrated campaigns. The study effectively reinforced the original core message of

Consumer Direct: online advertising has become a key driver of offline purchases.

Over time, Yahoo! has also learned that it needed to offer marketers a greater variety of online inventory than was available within its own portal. Despite its enormous reach and number of page views, Yahoo! could not always connect marketers to everywhere their consumers were. Even Yahoo! needed to stretch its advertising solutions beyond just the properties it owned. To make that leap, Yahoo! has entered into advertising sales partnerships with companies such as eBay, Comcast, WebMD, Ziff Davis, Forbes, and Bebo. In these arrangements, Yahoo! serves as the primary marketing and sales channel for the other partners' online advertising inventory. In addition, Yahoo! has made acquisitions such as Blue Lithium, an advertising network, and Right Media, an online advertising exchange, that contribute additional nonportal inventory. The result is an extensive "owned and operated" network that gives Yahoo!'s advertisers broad opportunities to connect with their consumer targets.

Finally, Yahoo! has been a leader in creating integrated advertising solutions in categories that previously had little online presence. Take the example of its recent effort for Kellogg's Special K. Kellogg's wanted to create a digital experience for women interested in weight loss, where it could promote the health and lifestyle benefits of its Special K products. It also wanted this digital experience linked to offline media (TV and print, in particular) and to its packaging. With this guidance, Yahoo! developed a program around the call to action, "Search Special K at Yahoo!" Here, a custom-branded "Special K" placement at the top of Yahoo! search results steered consumers to

SpecialK.com. And once on SpecialK.com, consumers were exposed to interactive tools that enabled them to customize their own Special K Challenge and connect with a community of weight managers and other women interested in weight loss. At the same time, SpecialK.com also featured content about the brand's cereal, protein wafers, and bars.

A REFRAIN OF CONSTANT CHANGE

By 2010, media and advertising offerings will be even more engaging, personalized, and interactive than they are today. Certainly not everything will be new: television will remain an engaging and popular medium; people will not stop reading magazines and listening to the radio. But it is every bit as true that media and advertising vehicles not yet imagined will have a powerful impact on both consumer behavior and marketer spending.

For media companies everywhere, the future will be about acquiring new skills and developing new relationships. They will have to learn to use their digital assets to create deeper, higher-impact experiences for both advertisers and consumers. At the same time, they will have to develop strong relationship marketing and experiential marketing capabilities to enable the kinds of targeted consumer dialogue and lead generation that marketers crave.

With more opportunities to collaborate directly with marketers, media companies will also need new go-to-market structures with clearer points of contact and differentiated sales and marketing services functions. And as the distinction between above-the-line and below-the-line spending disappears, media companies will have to rethink their portfolios, their planning frameworks, and their conceptions of effectiveness.

The playbook to prosper in the always-on era is indeed becoming clearer for media companies. They'll connect with consumers, with greater relevance and interactivity across more and more media platforms. They'll bring more insight, data, and analytics to inform their own decision making and that of their clients and partners. And they'll adopt more of a marketer mindset, articulating precisely how their media can drive results.

As these developments unfold, Mr. X's "only game in town" mentality will recede further and further from memory.

RESOURCES

➤ Gillin, Paul, *The New Influencers: A Marketer's Guide to the New Social Media*, Quill Driver Books, 2007.

➤ Jenkins, Henry, *Convergence Culture: Where Old and New Media Collide*, New York University Press, 2006.

➤ Kelly, Lois, *Beyond Buzz: The Next Generation of Word-of-Mouth Marketing*, AMACOM, 2007.

➤ McConnell, Ben, and Jackie Huba, *Citizen Marketers: When People Are the Message*, Kaplan Business, 2006.

➤ Scott, David Meerman, *The New Rules of Marketing and PR: How to Use News Releases, Blogs, Podcasting, Viral Marketing and Online Media to Reach Buyers Directly*, Wiley, 2007.

➤ Sernovitz, Andy, and Guy Kawasaki, *Word of Mouth Marketing: How Smart Companies Get People Talking*, Kaplan Business, 2006.

➤ Verklin, David, and Bernice Kanner, *Watch This, Listen Up, Click Here: Inside the 300 Billion Dollar Business Behind the Media You Constantly Consume*, Wiley, 2007.

➤ Weber, Larry, *Marketing to the Social Web: How Digital Customer Communities Build Your Business*, Wiley, 2007.

➤ For more resources and up-to-date information, see www.businessfuture.com.

4

METRICS: MOVING FROM IMPRESSIONS TO IMPACT

IT IS OBVIOUS THAT advertising has value for marketers only if it influences their target consumer's behavior. And marketers recognize this. In one recent survey, 90 percent of marketers across nine industries (see Exhibit 4-1) gave a resounding and overwhelming yes to the question: Is measuring effectiveness an important issue for you?

But the measurement of advertising effectiveness has long been a frustrating and imperfect science. Absent substantive measurement standards, marketers mostly sprayed and prayed—that is, they tossed out messages in various directions and hoped that some indication of consumer response would appear.

In television, this response usually translated to notations in the diaries that the media research firms paid a small

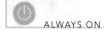

EXHIBIT 4-1 IS MEASURING MARKET EFFECTIVENESS AN IMPORTANT ISSUE FOR YOU?

Category	Percent
Auto	96%
CPG	89%
Financial Services	94%
Health	93%
Manufacturing	78%
Professional Services	85%
Retail	88%
Technology	100%
Telecom	85%
TOTAL	90%

Percent of Respondents Answering Yes

Source: Booz Allen Hamilton ANA

sample of the viewing audience to keep. Audience diaries, which record viewers' programming choices, use viewing behavior as a proxy for advertising value and impact—a very limited proxy. To be sure, the diaries have had one major benefit: they enable media researchers to extrapolate the size of the viewing audience and establish a baseline and a currency by which marketers, media companies, and agencies can transact business.

THE DEMAND FOR METRICS

As unsophisticated and unreliable as the traditional media measurement approaches may have been, they did provide standards and currencies that enabled marketers, buying agencies, and media companies to transact business. Today, however, this imperfect equilibrium no longer works because marketers are demanding more effectiveness and efficiency from their media buys. Digital media are reaching critical mass with consumers. And the promise of more granular (even real-time) data capture of consumer response to advertising is tantalizingly close to realization.

The transition to a new kind of advertising metric has had several consequences. First, the proliferation of media and the fragmentation of audiences have rendered the traditional currency of advertising—audience exposure or "reach"—a much less compelling measure of media value than it was before.

Second, the prospect of new metrics has contributed to the popularity of digital media among advertisers. The data and metrics provided by digital media potentially fulfill

"Virtually since television flickered into America's living rooms more than half a century ago, advertising time on it has been sold on the basis of audience size translated into gross rating points and CPM (cost per thousand impressions)," explains David Verklin, CEO of Carat Americas and chairman of Carat Asia-Pacific, the world's largest independent media buying agency. "But lately marketers have become less interested in the number of eyeballs that see a screen or hands that touch a page and more interested in the behavior of the owners of those hands and eyes, and how the ad message connects with them."

two pressing needs: to measure the efficacy of their efforts and to concentrate marketing resources only on those consumers who are interested in specific categories, products, or brands. Whether in "heavy-consideration" categories like automobiles, travel, and personal finance (where consumers often ponder options and compare alternatives in depth before buying) or "impulse buy" categories like packaged goods, entertainment, and apparel (where an ad can more immediately lead to a sale), marketers can use digital media to deliver contextually relevant messages and product information to specific concentrations of potential customers. They can target only those consumers who are looking for a new Volvo, who are planning a ski trip to Deer Valley, or who are searching for organic baby food. And they can measure the actual results of those efforts instead of relying on extrapolated audience estimates.

"The most important thing that's changed in the past 10 years is the measurability of what we do," says American Express CMO John Hayes. "New channels are regularly emerging that allow us to understand what it is we're doing as it relates to acceptability within the marketplace. And we can do it with much faster turnaround."

Marketers like Hayes are no longer satisfied with media placements that merely elicit awareness or even consideration from consumers. They are demanding far more substantive measures of an advertisement's influence on consumer preferences, purchases, and loyalty.

This, indeed, represents a paradigm shift, and marketers understand the potential. Consider how rapidly marketers embraced Google's pay-for-performance advertising model. No longer do marketers just ask, "What

EXHIBIT 4-2 **METRICS INFORM AND IMPROVE THE PURCHASE FUNNEL**

Penetration	Key Marketer Concerns
Awareness	How can I capture the attention of target consumers?
Consideration	How can I get consumers to put my product or service on their shopping list?
Trial	What can I do to get these consumers to try it and to purchase my product or service?
Occasional	How can I deepen relationships with my customers?
Regular	How can I create more value for my customers and "lock in" their loyalty?

Source: Booz Allen Hamilton

is the cost of the GRPs (gross rating points) that we are buying?" They also want to know results: "How many on-line registrations did that advertisement generate?" or, "How many prospective consumers called the 800 number and then were converted into customers?"

Third, with digital media, the ability to track the relationship between advertising and sales has continually grown more sophisticated and precise. When consumer actions—from browsing to clicking on an ad to sharing information with a friend to buying a product—can be recorded and analyzed, marketers are better able to track how well a piece of specific advertising induces consumers to purchase products. Ultimately, marketers expect digital media to give them the metrics and insights needed to allocate media buys with real precision, Marketers often think of consumer relationships as a funnel leading to purchase and repurchase, and ultimately to brand loyalty (see Exhibit 4-2). The metrics of digital media, before long, should be able to tell them how well a video series or a Web campaign drives consumers down the "purchase funnel" from being interested in buying the product to building real brand preference.

But the media metrics for the new digital media environment are still uneven. In many cases, they lack the standardization to enable "apples to apples" comparison of advertising effectiveness across media sectors. Marketers, agencies, and media companies all agree that improvements in these metrics across all media are going to be essential; otherwise, it will be difficult to profit in an advertising market increasingly characterized by more choice. In fact, only more reliable media metrics can enable marketers to aggressively realign their media purchases (or, in industry parlance, their marketing mix) to the new patterns of consumer behavior. This need is the driving force behind the inexorable movement toward more reliable and comparable media metrics (see Exhibit 4-3).

To gain this improved insight, the users of metrics—media companies, agencies, and the major measurement and marketing suppliers—need to move beyond reach-and-frequency metrics and provide more action-oriented evidence of media's return on investment. This reality is

> A pivotal point for us was when we realized that reach and frequency and other passive measurements were not going to be sufficient because they did not reflect whether or not we were really engaging our customers. Without engaged customers, we are not going to get what we need in terms of business outcomes. We stopped looking at awareness as an important measure.
> —John Hayes, CMO,
> American Express.

EXHIBIT 4-3 MARKETERS NEED NEW METRICS

The ways in which marketers evaluate their campaigns are evolving from metrics defined around

- ➤ Reach, frequency, and traditional gross rating points

- ➤ Demographics (age, income levels, gender, location)

- ➤ Brand metrics (aided awareness, ad awareness, message association, brand favorability, purchase intent/consideration)

to metrics that are both behavior-specific and action-focused:

- ➤ Engagement: ad recall, session time, traffic-to-marketer Web site, measures of active attention to content, and "transference" (brand halo from media)

- ➤ Quality and concentration of audience (early adopter influence, word-of-mouth/pass-along measures)

- ➤ Impact on purchase behavior (went to store, trial, repeat purchasing)

- ➤ Actual viewership (uniques, click-throughs, downloads, commercial ratings)

---

driving marketing and media to more outcome-based metrics.

Outcome-based metrics are not an entirely new phenomenon. There has been a slow and steady transfer of marketing budgets from metrics-deprived mainstream media (above the line) to direct marketing and promotions (below the line) that allow results to be tracked with greater accuracy.

Until recently, many observers dismissed the growth in below-the-line spending as a phenomenon driven largely by retailers, who, they said, were using trade promotions to gain a greater share of the huge marketing budgets of major consumer packaged goods companies. That has been true to some extent, but the spending shift from above-the-line to below-the-line advertising is better explained by the fact that marketers can more easily measure and prove the value of below-the-line spending.

The new form of outcome-based metrics combines the experience from below-the-line media with technological innovations in measurement (especially around television and digital) and the emergence of other new forms of metrics. Not all media can, or ever will, match the direct-response metrics of Google. But the broad evolution of new metrics will drive profound changes in the practice and the culture of marketing and brand advertising.

New technologies will support an eventual shift in audience measurement from estimates to actual census data—in other words, to "real" rather than "projected" results. Take Nielsen Media Research, the reigning master of television viewing measures. Traditionally, Nielsen has captured home television viewing data from 12,000 households (about one-tenth of one percent of the estimated 112 million U.S. households with televisions) and then used that sample to project ratings for the whole country. In the not-too-distant future, set-top boxes and other devices built into digital television systems will provide data on every consumer viewing action across both programming and commercials. Marketers will ultimately have access to media and advertising response data that will be comparable in granularity and comprehensiveness to the data captured today at the retail point of sale.

Today, Nielsen is investing heavily in an ambitious "Anytime, Anywhere Media Measurement" (A2/M2) cross-platform initiative designed to increase the scale and accuracy of its consumer sample. This program will move the company more deeply into online, outdoor, and in-store media and will strengthen the quality of Nielsen's TV-derived data. At the same time, smaller players such as IAG Research and TNS Media Intelligence are launching innovative alternatives to Nielsen. Data will be gathered, before long, from mobile meters that track out-of-home television viewing, from Internet video downloads and streams, and from videos viewed in PDAs, cell phones, MP3 players, and other portable devices.

In this increasingly dynamic environment, new outcome-focused metrics will shift the focal point of advertising measurement from exposure to results. These metrics will include:

- ➤ *Commercial ratings.* Viewership of commercials rather than programming; consumer retention of commercial messages; the impact of positions in pods (sequences of commercials that air during a single programming break); and the overall design of pods.

- ➤ *Session quality, engagement, and consumer experience/ satisfaction.* Ads recalled per session or visit; time spent per session or visit; average sessions per user; and strength of brand recall.

- ➤ *Total viewing behavior.* Number of consumers accessing media brands across both offline and online platforms (a metric that is especially relevant for traditional media companies that are trying to increase their digital presence and for marketers who want to compare digital to traditional media performance).

➤ *Opt-in activity.* Online registrations; open rates; toll-free calls; and requests for information.

➤ *Consumer participation.* Viral activity, such as pass-along and referral rates; amount of interaction with branded content, such as uploads of brand content to personal sites; the time spent in branded interaction; and the net promoter score (the percentage of consumers who would recomment a product).

➤ *Sales impact.* Leads generated; store traffic; and volume lift at retail stores.

Many marketers are eager to use metrics like these to crack the code of multiplatform advertising and marketing ROI. In fact, nearly 70 percent of marketers in that recent Booz Allen survey identified improved ROI analytics—along with the consumer insights that they deliver—as the most desired of all marketing capabilities.

Still there is much progress to be made. As Jim Stengel, Procter & Gamble's global marketing officer, says of his own company's prodigious efforts at measuring its advertising results, "We have made a lot of advances . . . we understand the elements pretty well. And we're not bad at figuring out how they interplay. But we're not quite where I'd like us to be in terms of projecting specific results."

Marketers like P&G are committed to solving this media and advertising riddle in order to foster the revolution in media metrics over the next few years. The era of single media, reach-focused measurement will pass as marketers make a transition to cross-platform campaigns characterized by greater levels of digital media and below-the-line spending. The next era of audience measurement will focus on how new combinations of media and advertising—TV, online, and print, as well as video games, outdoor, mobile, shopper marketing, and many others—influence consumers and how well they can move consumers through the purchase funnel.

MOVING FROM EXPOSURE TO ENGAGEMENT

In the always-on world, consumer engagement is truly scarce. Media messages can be delivered any time, anywhere. But marketers want more than exposure to eyeballs; they want the kind of consumer attention and action that moves brands. Thus, marketers must always strive to discover those elusive combinations of media and advertising that connect with consumers and increase brand demand. New measurement approaches will reflect both the quality of the audience (Did the right consumer see the advertisement?) and the impact of the actual message (Did

Whether people watch or not is not a useful measure of anything. Exposure has very, very weak correlation with purchase intent and actual sales, whereas an engagement measure has high correlation and is closer to what really matters, which is brand growth and creating brand demand.

—Joe Plummer
chief research officer,
Advertising Research Foundation.

the advertising move the consumer emotionally, affect the consumer's attitude, or help engender a specific action like a trial or purchase?).

In their efforts to answer these questions, marketers are beginning to redefine the metrics that they use to evaluate media and messages. But redefining, much less measuring, the complex relationships between media, messaging, and consumers is an enormously challenging task. It has been hard for marketers, agencies, and media companies to agree on exactly what engagement actually means, as opposed to an impression. There are multiple points of view and several unresolved questions:

- Does engagement refer to the amount of time consumers spend with a given medium?

- Is engagement a measure of how well consumers recall the advertising they watch or read?

- Is engagement a proxy for consumer responsiveness to, and interaction with, advertising?

- Does engagement take into consideration the interplay between creative execution, the media placement, and the media brand environment?

To make the task of measuring engagement even more complicated, it is likely to depend on several external factors, beyond the advertisement itself. These may include the amount of audience multitasking; the level of competitive media spending; and even retail conditions, where, for instance, a heavy dose of complementary promotional activity can affect how well advertising achieves its desired result.

EXHIBIT 4-4 **THE NEW MEDIA MEASUREMENT MODEL**

Traditional Audience Research		Emerging Consumer Insight Focused Model
Demographics	▶	Behaviors, Interests
Impressions	▶	Engagement, Actions
Platform-specific	▶	Campaign-centric
Usage/Segmentation	▶	Purchase Funnel
Estimate	▶	Census

Source: Booz Allen Hamilton

As the mysteries of consumer engagement are solved, a new media measurement model is emerging that supports the shift in marketers' focus from exposure to impact (see Exhibit 4-4).

Despite these challenges, engagement is gaining traction as a media metric. In the spring of 2005, Turner Broadcasting System's Court TV (since rechristened "truTV") became the first media company to use engagement as a currency when it began offering advertisers a guarantee based on "engaged" viewers in addition to a conventional audience guarantee based on Nielsen ratings. It determined engagement levels by partnering with media researchers to provide specific ad recall and minute-by-minute ratings analyses against its programming. If engagement dropped below the promised level, Court TV agreed to compensate advertisers for the shortfall by providing additional advertising inventory.

Founded in 1999, IAG Research has become the standard for determining advertising effectiveness on television. IAG measures viewer response to advertising and programming across all broadcast and major cable networks. Syndicated IAG data are now used by leading advertisers such as Verizon, Toyota, and NBC-Universal. IAG recognized that there was a void in advertising performance measurement: Nielsen measured how many people had an opportunity to see an ad, but there was no real-time content-specific measurement of *the impact of those airings*. IAG invented a new measurement system specifically to fill that void. IAG measures the effectiveness of television commercials, product placement, commercial sponsorships, and in-theater commercials using its unique online consumer panel as the basis for its research and recommendations.

IAG's system is an immensely ambitious undertaking, a syndicated data company à la Nielsen or Arbitron running a panel 365 days a year. It covers every prime-time program on the five broadcast networks, 17 major cable nets, as well as Spanish language leaders Univision and Telemundo.

Early on it became apparent from the viewer response data that Program Engagement is strongly correlated to ad recall and ad attentiveness, a very specific and conclusive finding that had long eluded the industry. The business application for advertisers and networks was straightforward. TV programs with higher engagement scores provide superior media environments for commercials.

This approach has enabled the IAG engagement metric to become an accepted supplement to the Nielsen ratings. In 2006, the company crossed a major threshold in terms of market acceptance when NBC became the first broadcast network to use its engagement scores as an additional guarantee for advertisers. By the 2007 upfront buying season, many broadcast and cable networks were offering some form of engagement-type metric. The engagement metric is especially advantageous for television because it goes beyond simple counts of how many viewers are tuned to a channel. Instead, IAG Program Engagement scores reveal whether viewers actually paid attention to the ads that ran within the programming. With many networks facing declining ratings and downward pressure on the pricing of their advertising inventory, this metric provides them with an opportunity to protect—and, in some cases, potentially enhance—the value of their audiences. Viewing matters, but engagement matters more.

Exhibit 4-5 illustrates the way in which IAG's engagement-based TV ad rankings have quickly become an accepted feature in the always-on world. With its reports, IAG was able to show that Sepracor's sleep aid Lunesta was both the most recalled prescription drug ad *and* brand for the 2006–2007 TV season.

The current engagement measurement models for television are, however, not perfect. For one thing, there's the potential bias of survey participants who watch much more TV than the rest of the sample group. There are concerns that participants may also over-recall ads simply because they know they are going to be asked about them. And there is the issue of whether and how much the incentives researchers provide to surveyed consumers may further skew the results.

There is also a larger, more fundamental concern: How

EXHIBIT 4-5 IAG RESEARCH RANKS ADS

Top Six Most Recalled New Prescription Drug Ads (2006/07 TV Season)

Rank	Brand	Company	Ad Description	Recall Index
1	Lunesta	Sepracor	7-Night Challenge; luna moth flies over bridge and water and into people's home/tent. (:60)	155
2	Lunesta	Sepracor	7-Night Challenge; luna moth flies over a lake into couple's home, then onto woman's pillow. (:60)	153
3	Zyrtec	Pfizer	Story #43; clothes falls on woman, and she sneezes. (:45)	138
4	Rozerem	Takeda	Abraham Lincoln, talking beaver, man in suit, and man in diving suit at a bus stop; your dreams miss you. (:60)	134
5	Crestor	Astra-Zeneca	Man at fish market near ocean whose cholesterol is out of whack; his body splits into various sections. (:60)	124
5	Vytorin	Merck/ Schering-Plough	Plates of food shown next to shots of relatives such as Grandpa Bow and bowtie pasta. (:60)	124

Top Five Most Recalled Prescription Drug Brands (2006/07 TV Season)

Rank	Brand	Company	Ad Description	Recall Index
1	Lunesta	Sepracor	7-Night Challenge; luna moth flies over bridge and water and into people's home/tent. (:60)	218
2	Lunesta	Sepracor	7-Night Challenge; luna moth flies over a lake into couple's home, then onto woman's pillow. (:60)	212
3	Imitrex	Glaxo-SmithKline	Teacher at a children's play rehearsal disrupted by a migraine; purple cartoon monster appears and then deflates. (:60)	153
4	Rozerem	Takeda	Abraham Lincoln, talking beaver, man in suit, and man in diving suit at a bus stop; your dreams miss you. (:60)	147
5	Plavix	Bristol-Meyers-Squibb/ Sanofi-Aventis	Fireman Jim is a formidable man who could be stopped by a clot that is the size of a drop of water. (:60/:75)	141

helpful are audience recall and attention in determining marketing effectiveness? Clearly, IAG's offering is only the first step toward a reliable engagement metric. But the current approaches still have not fully addressed a hard reality: consumers can watch an ad and give it their undivided attention, but the resulting high rating says little of consequence about whether or not they will act on the message. Until that additional linkage can be made, the full promise of engagement as a media metric will remain only partially fulfilled.

And then there is the issue of the amount of change that the media and marketing ecosystem can absorb. If the primary driver of network economics becomes the engagement rankings of commercials, what impact does that have on the programming and brands developed by the networks? And if networks begin using their creative and promotional prowess explicitly to keep consumers watching commercials as opposed to programming, what impact will that have on the future of ad-supported television?

Despite these issues, the networks recognize that they need to adopt new metrics that better enable agencies and marketers to judge the effectiveness of advertising spending. The IAG and engagement metrics, even with their imperfections, address that need. And as Alan Wurtzel, president of research at NBC Universal, described, "This is one of many kinds of things we're trying to do. One size doesn't fit all. We are trying to develop an array of metrics. Nielsen is still the primary guarantee; engagement is the secondary guarantee."

Moreover, as usage of IAG's engagement metric has grown, Nielsen has not stood still. It has developed one alternative to IAG's survey and brand-recall approach.

Nielsen's commercial ratings system tracks not just how many people watched a show, but how many people watched a commercial itself. In practice, the initial implementation of Nielsen's commercial ratings system has been both complex and problematic. For example, all commercial ratings systems must address the growth of time-shifted viewing, a trend that has made the measurement of viewing audiences and the shelf lives of TV spots a far more difficult issue.

In 2007, Digital Video Recorder household penetration was about 17 percent and is expected to reach 50 percent by about 2011. With more consumers time shifting and ad skipping, marketers wanted to pay for only those eyeballs that actually viewed their commercials. Media companies, in turn, desired a system that ensured that they got credit for live eyeballs as well as time-shifted viewers. Thus, at the end of 2007, the industry settled on a new ratings definition for television. Dubbed "live plus 3," it was based on the finding that nearly all viewing occurs within three days of a live telecast.

Another complicating factor for Nielsen has been resistance to the new ratings system from some prominent media networks. The networks objected to one aspect of the proposed data stream for Nielsen's commercial ratings: it was designed to support one overall rating for all commercials in a given program, as opposed to individual ratings for each commercial. In addition, some cable networks, such as MTV, did not embrace the move to commercial ratings. Given the ad-skipping tendencies of younger consumers and the amount of repeated programming on their schedules, they were concerned that the value of their ad inventory would decline significantly with commercial ratings.

Nonetheless, as the 2007 broadcast and cable upfronts were completed, the television industry compromised on a new ratings metric known as C3 (an acronym meant to stand for the average commercial rating plus three days of DVR playback) as the standard for TV media sales. C3's tenure as an industry standard may, however, be short-lived. As Nielsen becomes more competent and comfortable with supplying granular commercial ratings on a marketwide scale, it is likely that the industry will migrate to the minute-by-minute ratings that both Madison Avenue and marketers appear to desire.

Some companies are already experimenting with this approach. Mike Pilot, president of sales and marketing for NBC Universal, summed up the logic for such a move when he announced the company's cable upfront deal with Starcom USA: "We made a commitment to our clients to offer better accountability and measurability based on the metrics that matter most to them. Our minute-by-minute deal for Bravo—the first deal NBCU has done based on this metric—is truly about partnership and learning together in the changing media industry."

A movement toward minute-by-minute ratings may ultimately be inevitable, but in the near term it would introduce more complexity to creative media buying and advertising sales. In a viewing environment that rates individual commercials, the efficacy of the TV spots developed by agencies and marketers—as opposed to the programming and brands of the networks—would become the primary driver of broadcast economics. This would effectively require the networks to use their creative and promotional prowess to keep consumers watching commercials. It also would mean that each individual time slot within each pod would potentially have its own unique value and price.

If and when that situation fully comes to pass, networks will face pressure to make choices about how they program the advertising in their shows. Resigned to the reality of widespread adoption of C3 in cable, Viacom has already signaled publicly that its MTV Networks will focus more on integrating advertising directly into its shows; it will also consider shortening ad pods as well as increasing the number of them to avoid revenue loss.

In addition to the moves Viacom is contemplating, networks could choose to run only the advertising in their shows that generates the highest commercial ratings. They could also create new pricing models around positions within advertising pods, where first and last positions would be priced at a premium because they deliver the greatest number of viewers; air-time adjacencies to proven advertising performers would become more desirable. It is also not a far stretch to imagine greater use of Internet-like scrolls and other rich medialike inventory on screen. Speculation aside, it is certain that more granular commercial ratings will make for a more labor-intensive and analytically driven advertising marketplace. Networks and agencies will need even more analytical time and computing power to manage an exponentially larger set of ratings data.

Finally, even the most sophisticated, foolproof system of commercial evaluation ignores one important factor: even if a viewer watches a spot and gives it his or her undivided attention, there's no proof that this rating says anything of consequence about whether the consumer remembers the brand, the message, or the offer.

The most important consideration for advertisers is to determine if a viewer actually pays attention to an ad. A commercial rating may reveal that a spot aired in front of a viewer, but it would not highlight the consumer's interest in the advertising or whether the commercial drove a consumer response.

METRICS FOR EVERY MEDIUM

Now that the cross-platform advertising campaign has become an accepted solution to both media proliferation and audience fragmentation, media metrics must work across platforms also. This means that marketers must be able to measure results for each category of media *and* to evaluate those results in combination with and comparison against every other media platform they use. For all the promise of digital media, this still remains a major issue for marketers. In fact, in Booz Allen's recent survey with the Association of National Advertisers, 62 percent of marketers surveyed said that they would spend more on digital media if better cross-platform metrics existed to gauge advertising effectiveness.

The first step in building accountability, interactivity, and targetability in every kind of medium is to assign a metric for each. This prerequisite is in various stages of completion in different media, but it is being aggressively pursued virtually everywhere. Witness the metrics initiatives of a few of the media research firms:

> ➤ *Online.* Nielsen/NetRatings has developed what it calls a "total" suite of metrics that includes total minutes, total sessions, and total page views for online media.

Nielsen's rival comScore has committed itself to a "visits-based" family of metrics, including total visits, average minutes of visits, average visits per visitor, and average visits per usage day. Either system can, in theory, provide for more accurate measurement of online advertising. The lack of a standard, however, is sure to create some confusion.

➤ *Video games.* Nielsen's GamePlay Metrics plans to use the company's National People Meter sample, which comprises the same households that provide TV viewing data, to harvest information on the use of video games. It will deliver metered video game usage and demographic data by game title, genre, and player platform for Microsoft's Xbox, Nintendo's Wii, and Sony's PlayStation.

➤ *Streaming video.* comScore's Video Metrix goes beyond traffic—the number of people who enter a Web site—to determine who stays online and watches the complete video content.

➤ *Mobile.* Nielsen is testing a lipstick-sized "solo meter" that will track consumer use of personal audio and video players. At the same time, Rentrak Corporation and Hi-wire are collaborating to measure mobile TV viewing. Their initiative will begin by tracking the total size of the audience for mobile TV delivered via cell phones.

➤ *Blogs.* Nielsen BuzzMetrics is analyzing insights and opinions in online discussions, opinions, experiences, recommendations, and word-of-mouth promotion.

➤ *Digital video recorders.* Nielsen's "active/passive meters" are tracking DVRs to measure time-delayed views of TV programming. Case in point: Nielsen's ranking for the 2007 season premieres showed that ABC's *Grey's Anatomy* picked up an additional 3.89 million viewers via time-shifted viewing.

➤ *Outdoor.* Nielsen Outdoor is developing a survey-based ratings system using GPS-enabled devices. Npods (Nielsen personal outdoor devices) will provide demographic data about outdoor—mainly, billboard—impressions, as well as when they occurred and how long they lasted.

➤ *In-store.* Arbitron, the leader in radio measurement, has combined its Portable People Meter with other survey resources, including shopper intercepts and a partnership with Scarborough Research, to track exposure to in-store media. Nielsen is working through a consortium of retailers, manufacturers, and media buyers to create a similar service.

➤ *E-mail campaigns.* The Interactive Advertising Bureau has refined the category definition by introducing a set of parameters that includes e-mail conversions, e-mail revenue, e-mail gross profit, unique e-mail opens, and total e-mail click-throughs.

EXTRA, EXTRA: NEWSPAPERS MOVE TO TOTAL AUDIENCE METRICS

It's common sense for media companies to embrace cross-platform metrics. But it's not always easy.

As the print runs of newspapers declined and their online sites grew more popular, the industry's leaders decided to create a new total-audience measurement metric. Their intent was sound: to counteract notions that newspaper audience levels are dropping and that the medium cannot reach younger readers.

Unfortunately, this initiative encountered major challenges before the ink dried. The new total audience metric did not make any real effort to distinguish between the quality of paid circulation audiences and those who access newspapers for free online. In other words, the metric effectively equated a consumer who checks the weather online with someone who has the newspaper delivered to his or her home. Without sufficient additional insights into the advertiser value and quality of free online readership, newspapers lacked the ammunition to counter the prevailing view (among advertisers, at least) that a paying, newsprint-reading consumer (albeit a readership that is in decline) remains more valuable than an online reader.

Further complicating the picture was the fact that the newspaper industry has not settled on a common standard for online audience measurement. Individual newspapers are still free to choose either Nielsen or comScore (which have different online ratings approaches) as their reported online audience metric. As a result, marketers and media buyers still lack a consistent and comparable way to assess the value of many online newspaper audiences.

Once metrics are standardized and in place for media platforms, the issue of comparability arises. To get paid by advertisers for connecting them to consumers across platforms, media companies need to be able to mix metrics—a complicated undertaking when neither the metrics nor the perceived value of consumers in analog, digital, and other environments allow for simple, linear comparison.

Television networks, for instance, have made more of their content available on broadband and, in doing so, have found additional viewers. In the fourth quarter of 2006, NBC Rewind, an online site that enables consumers to watch network shows, attracted about 5 million users. By May 2007, that number had doubled to 10 million. NBC research also revealed that viewers were sampling shows such as *Heroes* online before deciding to watch them on TV. In an effort to track and eventually monetize expanding cross-platform media consumption, NBC Universal has since introduced a total audience measurement tool that captures consumer viewership across all of the company's media outlets (including broadcast, cable, online, and mobile).

Similarly, ESPN has found that it needs a way to measure its consumer engagement across its various media

> "If you look at the future of audience measurements, where you are measuring exposure across television, mobile phones, and the Internet, you are going to want to go beyond the current sample."
> —David Poltrack, executive vice president, research and planning, CBS Television.

platforms. Ed Erhardt, president of customer marketing and sales for ESPN and ABC Sports, explains, "Advertisers are demanding and asking their agencies to provide solutions that match up with how their brand is consumed, how their media is delivered, and how their advertising is created and then placed." To meet that demand, ESPN is partnering with Nielsen to develop a new audience measurement model that addresses the consumer interplay across TV, broadband, and mobile.

Nielsen itself, the most venerable of the TV metrics masters, is experiencing new competitive pressure in today's fast-changing markets. The digitization of media is creating growth opportunities in media measurement for disruptive new players. And, as one Boston venture capitalist noted in reference to the media research pioneer, "Nobody likes a company that has too much power."

Indeed, the market for media measurement in the United States has become much more interesting since TNS—one of the top four global providers of marketing research services—recommitted itself to competing with Nielsen. TNS tried to compete against Nielsen in the United States in the 1980s and was forced to withdraw from the national market. Since then, it has become a leading provider of audience-measurement services in 24 countries across Europe and Asia.

Today, as marketers seek a more granular and accurate analysis of consumer media behavior, TNS is again positioning itself as an alternative to Nielsen in the United States. It may succeed this time for several reasons. For one, the company boasts deep expertise in the measurement and analysis of commercial ratings, which is much more integral to the buying and selling of television in international markets. In addition, while Nielsen has historically emphasized the measurement of programming, TNS's expertise is rooted in the measurement of commercials—analyzing the impact of pod positioning, pod composition and length, promotional inventory, programming lead-ins, and even creative product. Finally, TNS also has partnered with cable and satellite operators to use their set-top box data, which provide granular tracking of channels and advertisements—down to the smallest increments of time.

Leading marketers are two to five times as likely to have the metrics and capabilities needed to judge the effects of new media than their less successful competitors.

It is impossible to predict who will win this metrics race, but certainly advertisers who will use these data to learn more about consumers and improve their marketing ROIs will benefit.

PARADISE BY THE DASHBOARD

The pace at which new measurement techniques, metrics, and suppliers are emerging is unrelenting. In fact, there has been such an explosion in media and metrics that marketers are struggling with a near-term glut in data. This condition has made the appeal of the marketing dashboard stronger than ever.

A marketing dashboard is a decision-making instrument that organizes the most important information and the most critical brand metrics so they can more effectively influence judgment. "We really focus on the marketing dashboard of 30-plus metrics that we look at on a quarterly basis," says Keith Pardy, Nokia's senior vice president of strategic marketing, brand management, and consumer relationships. "We set precise targets for these measures and look at them holistically. And we ask ourselves: What's happening with our brand preference scores? What's happened to our user base? Have we brought in new people? What's happening to our retention? How much money are we investing in fixed marketing versus working media?"

Marketers with a history in database and relationship marketing have been among the early adopters and leaders in developing metrics dashboards to manage their businesses in the always-on environment. But many marketers still have work to do in this domain, especially as their media mix becomes more weighted toward digital. Only about 20 percent of the marketers surveyed by Booz Allen and the Association of National Advertisers actually have functioning metrics dashboards in place that include digital media. This minority of market leaders (as illustrated in Exhibit 4-6) also comprises the companies that are two to five times more likely to have the metrics and capabilities to judge the effects of new media than their slower-moving counterparts. As a result, the majority of marketers will have to play catch-up and determine the mix of metrics that best reflects the clearest impacts on their sales, profitability, and overall brand equity.

During her four-year-plus stint as Yahoo!'s marketing head, Cammie Dunaway pulled together a dashboard of metrics that "aggregates the success that we see in individual campaigns and ladders it up to broader business impact." She explains, "When I first came to Yahoo!, I realized

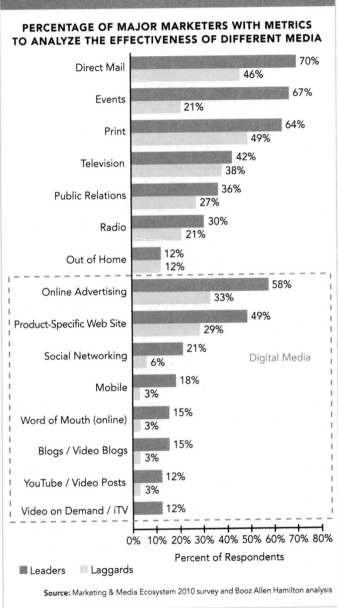

EXHIBIT 4-6 THE RACE TO NEW MEDIA METRICS

PERCENTAGE OF MAJOR MARKETERS WITH METRICS TO ANALYZE THE EFFECTIVENESS OF DIFFERENT MEDIA

Direct Mail — 70% / 46%
Events — 67% / 21%
Print — 64% / 49%
Television — 42% / 38%
Public Relations — 36% / 27%
Radio — 30% / 21%
Out of Home — 12% / 12%

Online Advertising — 58% / 33%
Product-Specific Web Site — 49% / 29%
Social Networking — 21% / 6%
Mobile — 18% / 3%
Word of Mouth (online) — 15% / 3%
Blogs / Video Blogs — 15% / 3%
YouTube / Video Posts — 12% / 3%
Video on Demand / iTV — 12%

Digital Media

0% 10% 20% 30% 40% 50% 60% 70% 80%

Percent of Respondents

■ Leaders   Laggards

Source: Marketing & Media Ecosystem 2010 survey and Booz Allen Hamilton analysis

how easy it is to lose the forest for the trees. I saw people being very accountable for the return on a specific piece of e-mail, for example, but not as knowledgeable as they should have been about how that effort contributed to the overall health of our business."

With the use of dashboards on the rise, it should come as little surprise that Google's analytics unit is offering advertising dashboards to any interested online marketer. Using the search company's metrics reports, online marketers can monitor their paid searches with a mix of dials, graphs, and other summary metrics. Important indexes for tracking a campaign's progress—items such as click-through ratio, total clicks, average cost-per-click, and total costs—are all presented in real time. And marketers can use the Google dashboard service to compare their key performance indicators to their competitors' performance. The presentation is clean, and the ability to make campaign adjustments based on dashboard-driven metrics is efficient. This may be a precursor of the next generation of media-oriented marketing dashboards.

Exhibit 4-7 shows how the Google dashboard zeroes in on the drivers of advertising impact for search marketing: traffic sources, site usage, sales opportunities, and revenue.

Google clearly has aspirations that extend beyond search. Its focus on dashboards is part of its strategy both to make marketing more efficient and to position itself as the interface to the marketer. To that end, in the fall of 2007, the company announced it planned to develop a "fully functioning marketing dashboard" that would aggregate marketer advertising performance across online and offline media.

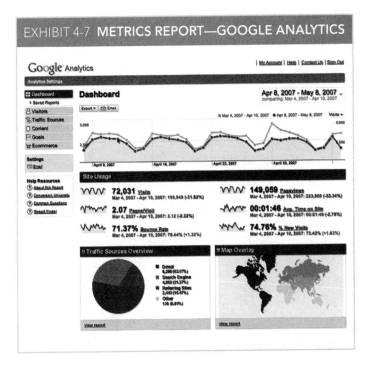

EXHIBIT 4-7 **METRICS REPORT—GOOGLE ANALYTICS**

WHO WILL BE
ADVERTISING'S BLOOMBERG?

In 1982, Michael Bloomberg created a revolution in the financial services industry. By providing financial professionals with a new set of tools, analytics, and data, Bloomberg L.P. transformed the way Wall Street worked. The key to that transformation and Bloomberg's runaway success was the way in which it made masses of complex data easier to access, report, analyze, and act upon. Specifically, the company created a "must-have" following by

➤ Organizing and structuring a mix of proprietary and third-party data and information

➤ Designing tools and analytics around the workflow of financial professionals

➤ Synthesizing the most critical metrics and market data on just two screens

➤ Emphasizing easy-to-use functionality

More than 25 years later, the marketing profession and its partners are asking many of the same kinds of questions Bloomberg was able to answer: Where do I find reliable information? Whom can I trust as a third-party source? Which metrics and analytics matter the most? As each day brings more and more data from more and more offerings, what tools can I use to sort through the clutter to find the insights I most need? And, perhaps most important, what's the most efficient way to put this information to work and improve the return on my marketing investment?

In much the same way that electronic information exchanges revolutionized the debt and equity markets in the 1980s, so too has digitization provided the stimulus that will alter the way marketers learn about the efficiency and efficacy of their advertising. Advertisers are eager to find the tools that can help them manage and make sense of data from across their entire marketing mix, and can help all of their partners gain more and better insight into how their current and prospective consumers are connecting with their brands.

Is any metrics provider poised to become the Bloomberg of advertising? Certainly there are many contenders. These include established players, whose expertise and resources would make them likely candidates—Google, Nielsen,

Microsoft, SAP, IBM, and TNS all come to mind. But, with so rich a prize at stake, there also will be many entrepreneurs and venture capitalists who see the opportunities inherent in developing a more efficient way to turn raw consumer data into actionable marketing insight.

At the front end of marketing planning, these new metrics will mean greater accuracy in judging consumer behavior, more finely tuned objectives, and less waste in budgeting. At the back end, marketers will be better able to estimate the degree to which their specific brand objectives have been met. With that information in hand, they will develop improvement measures, step up R&D, and work with consumers more effectively than they ever have in the past. For their part, the media companies will have the tools they need to price and design their offerings more effectively, based on a broader range of results and objectives.

The granular, outcome-based metrics that will enable these changes will become the key guideposts of marketer, media company, and agency decision making in the always-on world. Once they can manage with the knowledge of what actually works, they will be able to unlock new levels of creativity and insight, better connect with their consumer, and grow their businesses.

RESOURCES

➤ Ambler, Tim, *Marketing and the Bottom Line: The Marketing Metrics to Pump Up Cash Flow*, Financial Times, Prentice Hall, 2003.

➤ Dearlove, Des (ed.), *Results-Driven Marketing: A Guide to Growth and Profits*, strategy+business Books, 2005.

➤ Parris, Paul W., Neil T. Bendle, Phillip E. Pfeifer, and David J. Reibstein, *Marketing Metrics: 50+ Metrics Every Executive Should Master*, Wharton School Publishing, 2006.

➤ Wrenden, Nick, *ProfitBrand: How to Increase the Profitability, Accountability, and Sustainability of Brands*, Kogan Page, 2005.

➤ Young, Antony, and Lucy Aitken, *Profitable Marketing Communications: A Guide to Marketing Return on Investment*, Kogan Page, 2007.

➤ For more resources and up-to-date information, see www.businessfuture.com.

5

MARKETERS TO AGENCIES: "CHANGE OR DIE"

ADVERTISING AGENCIES were long considered the undisputed masters of brand messaging, communications planning, and media execution. Whether the challenge was launching, extending, or repositioning a product line or brand, agencies were the principal connection to consumers for marketers and their primary resource for brand strategy development and advertising execution. But changes in consumers' media consumption and shopping behavior have radically altered the relationship between marketers and agencies, especially for those agencies of record responsible for large, multidimensional campaigns.

Today's marketers expect much more from their agency partners than they ever did in the glory days of Madison Avenue. Their wish list includes

- Campaigns that are integrated across the media and communication channels that matter most to consumers

- Digital advertising know-how, and insight into consumer behavior, to support breakout marketing innovation

- An accountability focus that aligns marketing and advertising spending to business results, irrespective of platform

- Unfettered access to an agency's best talent, no matter where those executives may be assigned and what department or business unit they work within

And yes, marketers still also expect great creative output from their agencies.

Given the state of marketer-agency relationships, it is clear that these expectations are not being met. In a recent survey conducted by the CMO Council, a nonprofit group of senior marketing and brand decision makers, 64 percent of marketers reported that they had fired at least one agency in 2006—with public relations, Web design and development, and advertising at the top of their list of problem areas. The reasons for the dismissals: "Poor performance, lack of strategy and creative firepower, and insufficient outcomes." More than half of these same marketers also said they expected to make further revisions to their agency roster within the next year.

Exhibit 5-1 illustrates the tumultuous nature of marketer-agency relationships in 2006: nearly two-thirds of all relationships changed course in a single year.

Jerri DeVard, senior vice president of marketing and

EXHIBIT 5-1 AGENCY TURNOVER, 2006

AGENCY RELATIONSHIP CHANGES IN 2006

Category	Percentage
None	36.0%
Public Relations	35.7%
Web Design and Development	21.0%
Advertising	20.5%
Branding and Imaging	15.6%
Direct Marketing	7.8%
Interactive Marketing	7.8%
Events/Experiential Marketing	7.7%
Demand Generation	5.9%
Hosted Services/Solutions	5.5%
Special Programs	5.0%
Other	4.6%
Other Sales Promotions	1.4%

(64%)

REASONS FOR AGENCY CHANGES IN 2006

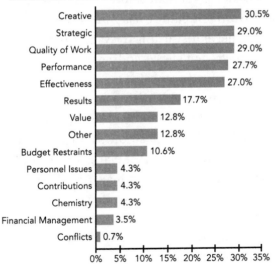

Category	Percentage
Creative	30.5%
Strategic	29.0%
Quality of Work	29.0%
Performance	27.7%
Effectiveness	27.0%
Results	17.7%
Value	12.8%
Other	12.8%
Budget Restraints	10.6%
Personnel Issues	4.3%
Contributions	4.3%
Chemistry	4.3%
Financial Management	3.5%
Conflicts	0.7%

Source: CMO Council, Marketing Outlook 2007

brand management at Verizon Communications until early 2007, didn't mince words on her assessment of agency performance: "They're evolving too slowly. They are holding onto the past and trying to rationalize it." A growing number of advertising professionals agree. "The CMOs have been screaming that they want something different, but the message has just filtered down to the brand teams in the last year," one agency principal told us in 2007. "The last year has been a watershed year. The advertising-agency model of the twentieth century simply doesn't work in the twenty-first century."

This isn't the first time that the agency model has required a fundamental shakeup. If we examine the value propositions that have driven the advertising industry since its inception, we can see that it has reinvented itself several times. And to its credit, it has always come out of the process stronger than before. In the process, the prevailing advertising culture has gone through three different stages, never discarding the value propositions of the previous stages but always adding to them. And it is now embracing a fourth proposition.

Proposition 1.0, which drove the advertising industry's first seven decades (from the 1880s through the 1950s), was basically a sales proposition. The agency promised to reach consumers on behalf of marketers through emerging mass media (newspapers, magazines, television) with straightforward, no-nonsense slogans and functionally focused, testimonial-driven messaging. The message to consumers was direct and simple: "This product gives you what you need."

With Proposition 2.0, which evolved during the so-called "Creative Revolution" of the 1960s, agencies like

Leo Burnett, Doyle Dane Bernbach, and J Walter Thompson began to practice a more nuanced form of persuasion. They promised to entice consumers to a brand through a seductive mix of jingles, brand characters, and smart copy if their agencies were put in charge of the marketing process. "We intrigue you, entertain you, make you think and feel good. Remember us. Trust us." was the tone of the agency's conversation with consumers.

Though Proposition 2.0 was known for its agencies that focused on great creative, the original full-service advertising agency of Proposition 1.0 also thrived—and even expanded—during this era. As Sir Martin Sorrell, chairman of WPP plc, the world's second largest media and communications services conglomerate, recently recalled:

> In the 1960s if you visited . . . JWT [then, J Walter Thompson] in Berkeley Square, London, you would find a creative department, a marketing department, an account-handling department, a media department, a public relations department. There would be a merchandising department, a direct mail department, a packaging department, a production department, an experimental film department, a market research department, a conference department. Even a home economics department with two fully equipped kitchens—plus an operations research department. . . .

By organizing all these disparate departments under one roof, Sorrell argued, the advertising agency could provide its clients with all the services necessary to develop and implement a marketing strategy from start to finish.

This same logic established a conceptual rationale for the era of mega-agencies—large advertising conglomerates formed through multiple acquisitions and mergers—that began in earnest in the 1980s. The first was Saatchi and Saatchi (where Sorell himself was financial director between 1977 and 1985). This created the road map for other mega-agencies such as WPP, Omnicom, the Interpublic Group, and Publicis. These organizations focused on creating the scale and footprint that they believed was essential to serving multinational marketers; they rolled up independent ad agencies around the world and a wide variety of marketing services firms. And as the mega-agencies consolidated their positions, they began to control ever larger shares of the overall advertising business.

The transition to a third proposition was now underway. It picked up speed in the 1980s and 1990s as marketers demanded both specialization and globalization at once from the mega-agencies. As the marketing mix grew more varied and the full-service agencies were compelled to deliver greater levels of both sophistication and efficiency, they also began to unbundle some offerings. This enabled clients to pick and choose their creative media buying and planning among other services, as if from a menu. The media planning and buying function was the first to be separated into a standalone service. At the same time, new specialty firms emerged around areas such as direct marketing, public relations, promotions, ethnic marketing, event marketing, and interactive advertising.

Proposition 3.0, in full swing by the late 1990s, promised marketers more in-depth expertise on an à la carte basis, wherever in the world they did business. It told marketers, "You can trust the advertising business to be the best in breed. We are as specialized as you need us to be, in every distinct area." At the same time, marketers were moving toward greater levels of integration—drawing together traditional and digital media, above- and below-the-line offerings, and planning plus creative functions. In other words, the specialist agencies often imposed higher levels of cost and complexity on their clients. Furthermore, their advertising solutions were too often optimized for individual media silos and not integrated sufficiently with other elements of the marketing mix.

The mega-agencies of Propositions 1.0 and 2.0 and the specialists of Proposition 3.0 all continue to grow. Since 2000, for example, revenues at the top five agencies worldwide have risen by 74.7 percent (see Exhibit 5-2). But neither the large nor the small agencies have consistently demonstrated that they can deal effectively with marketers' new demands for the always-on world.

Thus, as marketers focus more intently on digital media, measurable results, and integrated services, Proposition 4.0 has begun to emerge. It promises marketers relevance across the most critical consumer touchpoints. It focuses on helping them grow their businesses, not just manage their advertising. It is accountable, interactive, integrated, and targeted. To consumers and marketers together, Proposition 4.0 says, "We are all in each other's world. The more we know each other, the more helpful, relevant, and entertaining the marketing and advertising of products and services can be."

Today, virtually all agencies are under enormous pressure to restructure themselves to deliver Proposition 4.0. And some mega-agencies and innovative smaller shops are stepping up to the challenge. But Proposition 4.0 has

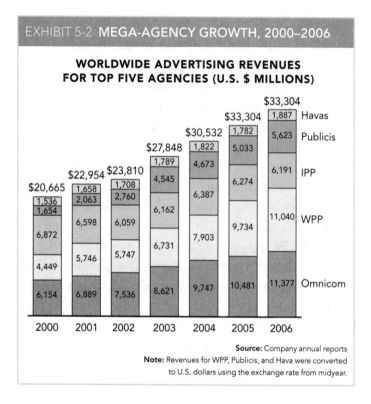

EXHIBIT 5-2 **MEGA-AGENCY GROWTH, 2000–2006**

**WORLDWIDE ADVERTISING REVENUES
FOR TOP FIVE AGENCIES (U.S. $ MILLIONS)**

2000	2001	2002	2003	2004	2005	2006	
$20,665	$22,954	$23,810	$27,848	$30,532	$33,304	$33,304	
1,536	1,658	1,708	1,789	1,822	1,782	1,887	Havas
1,654	2,063	2,760	4,545	4,673	5,033	5,623	Publicis
6,872	6,598	6,059	6,162	6,387	6,274	6,191	IPP
4,449	5,746	5,747	6,731	7,903	9,734	11,040	WPP
6,154	6,889	7,536	8,621	9,747	10,481	11,377	Omnicom

Source: Company annual reports
Note: Revenues for WPP, Publicis, and Hava were converted
to U.S. dollars using the exchange rate from midyear.

yet to be fully embraced by the advertising industry. And for good reason: the requirements for change are not incremental but transformational.

THE BARRIERS TO CHANGE

Why are advertising agencies having problems making the transition to Proposition 4.0? There are several changes to assimilate: the new importance of media planning, the demand for accountability and marketing ROI, the organizational challenges implicit in a new value proposition, and the emergence of a new wave of competitors.

The Media Planning Platform

Many agencies have been too slow to recognize just how much of their actual value to marketers has shifted from "the big creative idea" and "the most efficient media buy" to "the most sophisticated and innovative media planning." In the always-on world, the interdependencies between the media and the message have never been more important. The planner (*not* the creative or the buyer) has in fact become the driving force in today's marketing. It is the planner who chooses among media distribution platforms, who ensures that creative executions are integrated across the right touchpoints, and who leverages insights into consumer behavior to support advertising with more relevance and impact.

One of the greatest challenges for many agencies is the legacy of Proposition 3.0, when media planning was unbundled from creative. In many cases, even when agencies have recognized this shift, their response times have been sluggish. Many creatively focused shops still lack adequate

> Today, advertising agencies are rapidly building back that [planning] capability, recognizing that they have to be masters not just of the creative message, but of the ability to connect with consumers. They realize that if consumers are consuming influence differently and are influenced differently, they'll be marginalized if they don't understand those processes. We want a holistic-consumer-connection planning capability.
>
> —Rob Malcolm, president, global marketing, sales, and innovation, Diageo PLC.

planning capabilities and the resources to strengthen them. Many media buying and planning agencies, driven by a business model based on volume and profitability, have underinvested in new planning approaches. But respond they must; their clients are clamoring for better counsel about the impact of media on the effectiveness of advertising.

Many marketers—an impressive 76 percent of them, according to a recent Booz Allen/Association of National Advertisers study—feel strongly that creative and media planning need to be rebundled. And there are outspoken advocates for a new planning priority within the agency community itself. As Shelly Lazarus, Ogilvy & Mather's chairperson and CEO says, "It's the planning part that needs to come back to where the initial thinking is being done."

The Demand for Accountability

Like their clients, agencies are struggling to get a grip on the effectiveness of marketing spending. For years, too many in the advertising industry have balked at making investments in the new measurement techniques, research, and ROI analytics needed to better demonstrate the efficacy of their campaigns to their clients. Now, although cost pressures challenge their economics, they have no choice. Marketers are demanding it.

As Olaf Göttgens, vice president, brand communications, says of the marketing efforts at Mercedes-Benz Passenger Cars, "There is only one indicator that really counts: the amount of money spent on marketing for each car purchased."

The demand for ROI and accountability is also coming from marketing procurement executives, and often the chief financial officer. For years, the corporate procurement function has steadily exerted more control over marketing expenditures and supplier relationships. For agencies, the growing prominence of procurement in the sales process has created new gatekeepers, reinforced an emphasis on getting "more for less," and converted many hard-won client relationships to the open competition of an RFP.

Exhibit 5-3 illustrates the degree to which marketers, who are facing mounting pressure to measure and demonstrate the effectiveness of their spending, are passing that pressure through to their agencies.

Organizational Challenges

Agencies, especially mega-agencies, face tremendous organizational challenges in the shift to Proposition 4.0. This value proposition requires that agencies reinvent their go-to-market structure and offerings and discover how they can create stronger connections to their clients' key consumers. In doing so, they must seriously reconsider their traditional approaches to talent management, compensation, and account management.

Many agencies have been stymied by their own internal systems. Among the common problems are talent management and compensation systems that emphasize individual business unit performance and, thus, encourage the competitive divisions that still exist within the mega-agencies. Additionally, there are the budget processes that create fierce infighting over funding between business units.

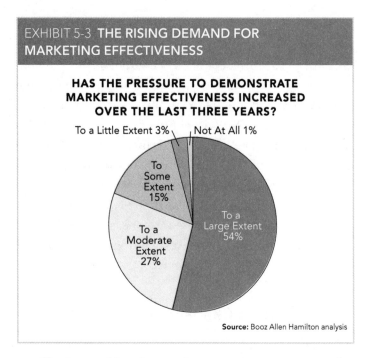

EXHIBIT 5-3 THE RISING DEMAND FOR MARKETING EFFECTIVENESS

HAS THE PRESSURE TO DEMONSTRATE MARKETING EFFECTIVENESS INCREASED OVER THE LAST THREE YEARS?

To a Little Extent 3% — Not At All 1%

To Some Extent 15%

To a Moderate Extent 27%

To a Large Extent 54%

Source: Booz Allen Hamilton analysis

The internal barriers to change are even more complex given the large geographic footprints and many differently branded business units that exist within mega-agencies. Often, acquisitions have been stacked one on top of another in these holding companies, and internal issues of infrastructure, decision rights, and change management have never been fully resolved.

For these companies, the transitions required to move from independence to collaboration to integration remain a major challenge. As WPP's Sorrell explains, "The biggest problem our clients face—and that we face internally within WPP—is the inability of people to work together. You have a coordination problem when you have two people in an organization; when you have 97,000, you can imagine what a nightmare it is, particularly given the structure."

The urgent need for talent is an internal barrier in and of itself. Agencies, big and small, simply have not been attracting the level and quantity of talent required to respond to marketers and consumers in Proposition 4.0.

For decades, agencies relied on the promise of sexy, creative-oriented work as a primary talent lure, even in the face of relatively low compensation. But young workers today have many more options for the same kind of professional gratification. The agencies appear to be losing the latest war for talent; the most capable young businesspeople, rather than considering traditional advertising for a career, are being hired by digital companies, media players, consulting firms, and software companies, not to mention a wide variety of start-ups. A strong case can be made that a successful career in advertising is more likely to be found inside the Google-plex or the garages of Silicon Valley than on Madison Avenue.

This increased competition, for both management and creative talent, has created a skills deficit that has left agencies vulnerable on several key fronts. Without access to leading digital insight, they are threatened with the loss of high-growth business opportunities to specialist teams and technology-savvy competitors—a problem that will become more acute as marketers devote larger shares of their budgets to new media such as broadband and mobile. Absent top analytical strength and strategic talent, which is typically sourced from leading MBA programs, agencies will also be challenged to provide the most meaningful business counsel to their clients' senior executives.

There is a similar dearth of talent in the leadership pipeline at many agencies. At the big agencies, the majority of senior-level copywriters and art directors remain digital

IN THE KELLOGG, Columbia, Wharton, Stanford, and Harvard MBA classes of 2006, less than 1 percent of graduating students joined the advertising industry. Five percent signed on with media or Internet services companies, 6 percent with consumer goods companies, and 26 percent with management consulting firms.

immigrants, not natives. The skills that they developed and perfected for television and print do not transfer easily to social networks, video games, mobile phones, and the like.

"The biggest gap is senior leaders with digital experience," says one agency executive. "To provide direction, our creative people need relevant digital experience. And they don't have it." Nor is this lack of digital experience a secret to marketers. A study by Evalueserve for Sapient, a global interactive agency, found that only 10 percent of the CMOs surveyed in the United Kingdom and the United States reported that they would "seek to partner with large advertising agencies for their online marketing."

THE DIGITAL PERSUADERS AND THEIR WEAPONS OF MASS DISRUPTION

The final and perhaps greatest challenge that agencies face in the emerging Proposition 4.0 environment is a host of new, aggressive competitors. There is an enormous set of digital enterprises that have spotted significant growth potential in the $600 billion global advertising industry.

While each of these companies has its own strategic agenda, they all share a common vision: they recognize that advertising is moving toward solutions that are more digital, automated, targeted, customized, data-driven, real time, interactive, and measurable. In short, they know that the future of advertising has probably more to do with the user interfaces and algorithms of software engineers than it does with the skills and practices of traditional agency executives.

With their innovative offerings and acquisitions, major technology-based players, such as Google, Yahoo!, Microsoft, and AOL, are a very real and active threat to agency hegemony. These companies are accustomed to moving with great speed. They are pushing for global scale, with analytic and technological capabilities well beyond the scope of most agencies. And they are building virtual warehouses stuffed full of the consumer-centric data and insight that marketers crave. Most significant, they are developing end-to-end digital advertising platforms centered around ad servers such as Atlas or Doubleclick. For an example of this type of new digital media marketing value chain, see Exhibit 5-4. These types of operators put the ad servers (rather than the agencies) on the strategic high ground to

> Develop direct relationships with advertisers and marketers

> Determine how advertising economics (such as commissions) are shared among participants

> Manage how ads are placed and bought

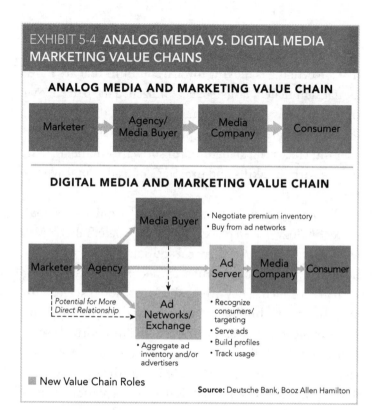

EXHIBIT 5-4 ANALOG MEDIA VS. DIGITAL MEDIA MARKETING VALUE CHAINS

ANALOG MEDIA AND MARKETING VALUE CHAIN

Marketer → Agency/Media Buyer → Media Company → Consumer

DIGITAL MEDIA AND MARKETING VALUE CHAIN

Media Buyer
• Negotiate premium inventory
• Buy from ad networks

Marketer → Agency → Ad Server → Media Company → Consumer

Potential for More Direct Relationship

Ad Networks/Exchange
• Aggregate ad inventory and/or advertisers

• Recognize consumers/targeting
• Serve ads
• Build profiles
• Track usage

■ New Value Chain Roles

Source: Deutsche Bank, Booz Allen Hamilton

> ➤ Build deep, data-driven consumer insight into actual behavior

Yahoo! and AOL already have demonstrated the willingness and ability to be pacesetters with offerings in the following areas: customizable rich media, such as Yahoo!'s Smart Ads; behavioral targeting, such as Yahoo!'s Blue Lithium and AOL's Tacoda; and advertising networks and exchanges, such as AOL's Advertising.com and Yahoo!'s Right Media. But it is the head-to-head battle between

Microsoft and Google for advertising assets, technological innovation, and management talent that will have the most powerful impact on the advertising industry.

Considering that Google has annual revenues approaching $17 billion and 34 percent market share of all global online advertising, it's hard to believe that the company began selling search-based advertising only in 2000 and did not go public until 2004. Today, it sells more online advertising than any other company in the world.

Google's paid-search model, which emphasizes catching consumers in "buying mode" and accountability metrics, has captured the media zeitgeist and attracted marketers from companies of all sizes. Its comparatively low-cost approach, ease of use (there's nothing complicated about text-based ads), and user-friendly automation for purchasing and managing online insertions has brought many millions of new dollars into the online advertising market—money that has also been diverted away from traditional media.

As shown in Exhibit 5-5, Google's advertising revenues grew by an astonishing 432 percent between 2004 and 2007 (74.6 percent compound annual growth rate). In addition, it has captured two-thirds of search-advertising spending and one-third of all online advertising.

To build an even more formidable position, Google is moving forward in four different directions simultaneously:

➤ It is using acquisitions, such as the $3.1 billion purchase of DoubleClick in April 2007 and the $1.7 billion purchase of YouTube in October 2006, to establish a stronger

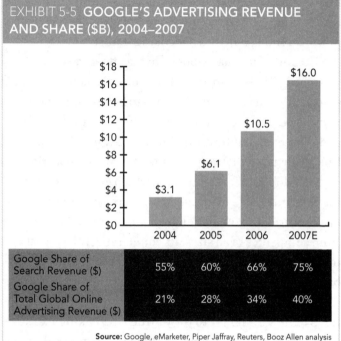

EXHIBIT 5-5 **GOOGLE'S ADVERTISING REVENUE AND SHARE ($B), 2004–2007**

	2004	2005	2006	2007E
Revenue ($B)	$3.1	$6.1	$10.5	$16.0
Google Share of Search Revenue ($)	55%	60%	66%	75%
Google Share of Total Global Online Advertising Revenue ($)	21%	28%	34%	40%

Source: Google, eMarketer, Piper Jaffray, Reuters, Booz Allen analysis

Note: 2007 estimate for Google based on consensus estimate analysis of FY2007 from Reuters.

presence in display or "banner" ads and rich media—the kinds of advertising that can be downloaded or embedded in a Web page.

➤ It is launching innovative new formats such as YouTube video units and Gadget Ads, portable applications that can be customized and packed with RSS feeds, video, and animation to make online venues more attractive to consumers and more useful to their sponsors.

➤ It is delivering the metrics and insight that support marketing accountability through continued investments in Google Analytics, which provides dashboards and metrics needed to increase the ROI of search campaigns, and Google Trends, which delivers consumer insight based on search term usage.

➤ It is pushing and agitating for more "openness" in mobile content and applications in the hopes of accelerating the growth of mobile advertising and the prominence of search within it.

At the same time, Google is actively working to "Googleize" more traditional media, most disruptively in the $60 billion U.S. television industry. While the company has experimented with radio, newspapers, and magazines, its tests with Echostar's Dish Network and local cable operators deserve attention for those who care about the future of advertising.

The goal of the Echostar experiment is to demonstrate that Google's model—auction pricing, focused targeting, and real-time results reportage—can make TV more valuable for marketers. In this test, Google provides the interface, marketplace, and insight. Every element of the advertising model inherent in the Echostar program has implications for the advertising and media industries. The auction approach introduces pricing transparency and automation into the buying and selling of TV spots. Google provides metrics showing how many consumers actually watch commercials, shifting the media currency from show ratings to commercial ratings. Marketers can use the resulting insight to determine if their ads are being watched. Implementation of Google's brand of more granular commercial ratings could drive dramatic changes in not just how media are planned (the process by which shows are selected by advertisers and their agencies) but also how creative is evaluated and developed (based on more direct metrics that reveal when customers are more likely to stay tuned).

Every few months, the search giant issues conciliatory statements suggesting that it has no intention of getting into the agency business. Yet Google remains the greatest single threat to agency disintermediation, and there is little doubt that it intends to change the industry landscape. As CEO Eric Schmidt told marketers via the *Wall Street Journal,* "Our long-term fantasy is we walk up to you and you give us say, $10 million, and we'll completely allocate it for you across different media and ad types."

Microsoft wants to be a leader in advertising as well, pledging publicly that advertising will contribute "25 percent of the company's business within a few years." The company has since set an additional goal of becoming number two and ultimately number one in online advertising during the next three to five years. Microsoft's strategic vision for advertising appears to be driven by three convictions: that the entire advertising market will eventually be digitized; that an advertising-based model is the most scalable model for digital businesses, as opposed to subscription-supported or pay per use; and that even software—the company's core business and cash cow—can one day be profitably delivered as an ad-supported service. To make this vision a reality, Microsoft believes that it needs to own one of what is likely to be a few preferred global digital advertising platforms (Google certainly being one of the others) for marketers as well as publishers.

In 2007, Microsoft demonstrated its commitment to the future of advertising by investing more in advertising-related acquisitions than it spent on overall R&D. In May of that year, Microsoft made its largest acquisition ever, paying $6 billion for aQuantive, Inc. The price represented a premium of about 85 percent on aQuantive's stock, but following Goggle's acquisition of DoubleClick, the deal was viewed by many as a critical strategic move for Microsoft.

aQuantive came with three major assets that have quickly become important incremental elements of Microsoft's overall advertising portfolio:

- *Atlas*, an integrated ad-serving and campaign-management platform, which enables Microsoft to sell advertising for sites other than its own, and to deliver video and rich media to them

- *Drive PM*, an advertising network that improves Microsoft's ability to offer a greater array of publisher inventory to marketers

- *Avenue A | Razorfish*, a reputable digital advertising agency that provides Microsoft with greater near-term access to and insight into marketer needs, as well as digital account expertise

Microsoft's portfolio also includes Windows Live (personal Internet services and software), MSN.com (the portal), and Microsoft AdCenter, the online advertising platform. In 2007 Microsoft further focused its attention on the high-growth advertising-networks sector with the acquisition of AdECN, an auction exchange for display advertising. That same year, it also purchased Screen Tonic, a

French firm which specializes in delivering location-based ads to mobile devices. This service complements Microsoft's positions in other emerging advertising platforms with high growth potential, such as video games.

Microsoft also moved decisively to outbid Google for a 1.6 percent stake in Facebook. Although in the near term this $240 million investment entitled Microsoft to little more than the right to sell remnant or "leftover" Facebook ad inventory internationally, it did link Microsoft directly to the most dynamic player in social networking—a mega-growth, Internet-based, younger-skewing "operating system" that has explosive potential for applications in advertising, messaging, video games, and mapping. And, with $22 billion in cash on its balance sheet and clear aspirations for global market leadership, it seems likely that Microsoft will focus even more on advertising-oriented acquisitions in the future.

THE DIGITAL ACCESS ROAD TO CREATIVE CONTENT

Need a good creative idea? Here are two innovative alternatives to traditional advertising agencies:

➤ Los Angeles–based *Spot Runner* offers a video bank of thousands of customizable spots that are ideal for today's local television stations and tomorrow's online video, VOD, and IPTV. By producing ads inexpensively (a Spot Runner video ad costs about $500), the company hopes to make TV advertising accessible to the many small businesses that cannot afford the cost of broadcast production. And like a full-service agency, Spot Runner provides end-to-end service: managing the media plan, the ad buy, and campaign reporting for its clients.

➤ *Openad.net* is a Slovenian-based digital marketplace that offers marketers in search of advertising and design ideas access to an international network of some 9,000 creatives, including freelancers and agency professionals. Openad.net's frictionless, low-cost, and borderless approach to sourcing creative talent doesn't appeal to just marketers with small budgets. In the summer of 2007, Gillette used Openad.net to solicit pitches from creatives in more than 21 countries before settling on Live 1, an Indian agency. Gillette then returned to Openad.net for ideas on how to translate Live 1's creative concept ("She knows the difference") into executions across TV, print, promotions, and digital.

PATHS TO PROPOSITION 4.0

The challenges and new competition in Proposition 4.0 notwithstanding, there is still a wide-open window of opportunity for agencies that are intent on surviving and profiting in the always-on era. In fact, the lessons from those agencies that are working to transform their businesses offer clues to how the entire advertising industry might look in the near future. Here are four agencies whose strategies and approaches are worth considering:

1. WPP, a global agency that is moving aggressively toward technology and non-advertising-based services

2. Publicis/Digitas, another global enterprise, which is industrializing and globalizing the production of digital ads

3. Crispin Porter + Bogusky, a Miami Beach–based agency that is reinventing creative for digital

4. Naked Communications, a London-based agency that is carving a global niche for itself by focusing on media strategy and media communications planning

WPP

To date, WPP, with its £5.9 billion in 2006 revenue, is the mega-agency that has been perhaps the most aggressive in transforming itself for Proposition 4.0. The company has long been a consolidator—rolling up well-known agencies, such as JWT in 1985, Ogilvy Group in 1989, Y&R in 2000, Cordiant in 2003, and Grey in 2005—and it appears committed to an acquisition-based strategy in the near term. In the process, WPP has expanded globally, developing a footprint in China, India, Latin America, the Middle East, and Eastern Europe, all locales in which marketing spending is likely to accelerate as economic conditions strengthen.

At the same time, through myriad smaller acquisitions and investment stakes, WPP has been expanding its marketing services menu, particularly in direct marketing, promotions, relationship marketing, public relations, market research, event marketing, and other specialist communications. In 2006, these services contributed 53 percent of WPP's revenue, and the company's objective is to build that up to 67 percent.

Sir Martin Sorrell's biggest response so far to the threat of Google and the promise of the future of advertising has been the $650 million acquisition of 24/7 Real Media in May 2007. This transaction put WPP squarely into the ad-networks and ad-serving businesses—and in head-to-head competition with Google/DoubleClick and Microsoft/aQuantive. Moreover, 24/7 Real Media also brought WPP valuable expertise in behavioral targeting, rich media, search marketing, and campaign management. It represented a defining move for WPP, aimed at owning the technology, innovation skills, and data that appear to be must-haves for an always-on digital future.

In addition, WPP has developed a sizable portfolio of minority positions in multiple digital businesses. As of this writing, it has made investments in targeted video advertising via Visible World, VideoEgg, and Spot Runner; social media via Live World and Visible Technologies; mobile via JumpTap, Iconmobile, and m:metrics; interactive via Blue, Schematic, Refinery, and Blast Radius; and video game advertising via Wild Tangent. Each represents an opportunity for the mega-agency to experiment with (and shape) emerging advertising platforms, as well as to provide a pathway to greater ownership if and when their promise materializes.

Through outright acquisitions and investment stakes in over 100 companies, WPP (Exhibit 5-6) has become a

EXHIBIT 5-6 WPP—THE FULL-SERVICE AGENCY
IN PROPOSITION 4.0

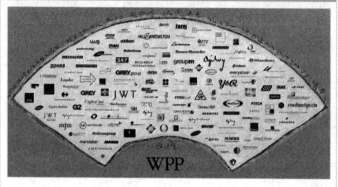

Source: WPP 2006 Annual Report

mega-agency with more than 2000 offices doing business
in 106 countries

Finally, WPP is working to address the talent management issues that have hampered the advertising industry
as it seeks to offer marketers more seamless and strategic
service. The mega-agency has been experimenting with
cross-business unit account teams that gather the resources needed to best serve a client from across all of the
group's various companies (Think Team Vodafone, which
comprises some 30 WPP agencies, including Enterprise
and JWT).

To recruit the best and the brightest, WPP has created
a marketing fellowship program designed to attract top
MBA prospects. These students are invited to spend three
one-year rotations within WPP companies, during which
senior executives, including board members, serve as
their mentors. The objective: develop high-caliber man-

agers who can work across a variety of marketing disciplines. Says Sorrell, "WPP is the only company in our industry to do this."

Publicis/Digitas

By 2006, the reality of Proposition 4.0 had hit hard at Paris-based Publicis Groupe. The mega-agency's lack of expertise in digital advertising was viewed as a major weakness. As chairman and CEO Maurice Lévy explained to the *New York Times*, "What we see is a massive, massive transfer of investment from traditional media to the Internet." In December 2006, Publicis responded by buying U.S. digital-marketing specialist Digitas for $1.3 billion.

Digitas is itself a good model for how agencies can reshape themselves to meet the new challenges and opportunities in the always-on world. Formed in 1999, Digitas was born from the merger of Bronner Slosberg, a major U.S. direct-marketing firm, and the Strategic Interactive Group, an interactive marketing firm. An early convert to Proposition 4.0, the new company focused on direct marketing, with a particular emphasis on database marketing, customer relationship management, and, ultimately, online marketing.

As online advertising expanded, Digitas was ready to respond. Using its direct-marketing model as a foundation, it created a dashboard-based platform that broke down online ads into measurable components and determined which pieces worked best for specific audiences. Digitas also created the Active Brand Experiences platform, which uses a consumer's personal data, such as age and location, to craft different messages each time he or she sees a product or service, from first exposure to the moment of purchase.

With services like these, Digitas attracted a roster of major clients, including American Express, Best Buy, Delta Airlines, General Motors, and Allstate. It weathered the 2001 collapse of the online advertising market better than most interactive boutiques. Then it acquired Modem Media, another digital creative agency, in 2004 and Medical Broadcasting LLC, a health communications agency, in 2006. By the time Publicis came courting in late 2006, Digitas had so well married technology-driven creative—for Web sites, online promotions, e-mails, rich media—to a strong focus on results-based metrics that it had become one of the largest independent digital agencies in the United States.

For Publicis, Digitas represents a critical component of its strategy to industrialize digital creative and develop creative executions cost-effectively, with sufficient scale for multiple platforms (television, print, mobile, and broadband). The Digitas deal is also a catalyst for building a global digital production line through low-cost, offshore labor in countries such as Ukraine, Costa Rica, India, and China. Publicis has since added Communications Central Group, the largest digital agency in China, to its portfolio and rebranded it Digitas Greater China.

Finally, Publicis's acquisition of Digitas offers a different perspective on how a mega-agency might prosper in the always-on era. Unlike WPP, which has chosen to compete directly with Google and Microsoft, Publicis is taking a different tack. As Maurice Lévy explained, "[Google] will have to make a choice between being a medium or being an ad agency, and I believe that their interest will be to be a medium. We will partner with them as we partner with CBS, ABC, Time Warner, or any other media group."

Crispin Porter + Bogusky and Naked Communications

If you've gotten the impression that only mega-agencies can compete in the always-on world, then consider two smaller agencies that prove size is less important than a relevant and imaginative range of advertising services. One is Miami's Crispin Porter + Bogusky, whose key clients include Volkswagen of America, Burger King, Coca-Cola, American Express, and Nike; the other is U.K.-based Naked Communications, whose clients include Marks & Spencer, Heineken, and Honda.

Neither agency describes itself in traditional terms. "'We're a factory," the Crispin Web site says, "a factory that makes ads." Naked emphasizes that it's a "communications *planning*" agency—with a sharp and distinct emphasis on media strategy and planning.

Crispin talks about its advertising and various communication tools as "products," and it has rebranded account management as "content management." While many established agencies dismiss the firm as a one-trick creative pony, marketers often see it as a modified flashback to Proposition 2.0: innovative creative output from a full-service agency that provides media planning and buying, research, public relations, and production services.

Crispin's winning pitch to Burger King (BK)—a massive account that an agency its size probably had no right to pitch—is a striking example of its eclectic approach. In its first meeting with the fast-food giant, the Crispin partners suggested that BK turn its tray liners into ad vehicles and change the signage in its restaurants. Before it ever pitched a traditional advertising idea, Crispin's team also rewrote the BK employee handbook to show how persuasive a consistent message could be throughout an organization.

Crispin best demonstrated its capacity to create the kind of relevant, attention-grabbing advertising that enables brands to interact with consumers in the always-on world by developing a series of video games that were sold in BK restaurants with the purchase of a Value Meal. These games, including "PocketBike Racer," "Big Bumpin'," and "Sneak King," connected with customers so well that they became hits in their own right. (See Exhibit 5-7.)

In just five weeks, the Burger King video game promotion created by Crispin Porter + Bogusky induced consumers to buy over three million games for $3.99 each with the purchase of a Value Meal.

Naked Communications believes that the future of media agencies will be determined by their ability to guide marketers through the increasingly complex Proposition 4.0 media landscape. To that end, it positions media strategy and planning at the heart of every brand strategy. It pitches itself to clients as a creative alternative to media agencies—organizations that have become too process-driven and planning-light.

Naked seeks to be a different kind of strategic adviser, working upstream on the development of advertising and media ideas that, often, someone else will implement. It's an aspiration that has the potential to position Naked as a highly valued integrator, not just determining the media

EXHIBIT 5-7 **POCKETBIKE RACER VIDEO GAMES BY BURGER KING** ®

buy but defining the size and shape of the media strategy and how all the pieces of the communications mix work together to drive results. Naked's approach is fundamentally media-agnostic; it doesn't seek to emphasize any one marketing, media, or advertising discipline. The firm's offering is supported by eclectic teams of talent, including media planners, management consultants, and even journalists, who come together to respond to the specific needs of each client.

A good example of Naked's approach is its work for Boots, the United Kingdom's largest pharmacy chain. In 2003, Boots employed a TV campaign to launch a new service designed to speed the filling of prescriptions by collecting them directly from doctors. The campaign sputtered. As an alternative, Naked very practically suggested that Boots tell customers about the service while they were standing in line waiting for prescriptions. The in-store program was conducted by Boots's employees. It spoke directly to the 16 million consumers who visited Boots locations every week and increased the number of consumers participating in the service by "several hundred percent at a fraction of the cost of a TV campaign."

In April 2007, Naked further refined its planning focus with the launch of Naked Numbers. The new service fuses established measurement techniques, such as econometrics, with digital tracking tools. Its goal: to offer clients a way of measuring campaigns that integrate traditional media channels with more unconventional marketing activities.

As with Crispin, some traditional agencies initially dismissed Naked's market positioning as little more than posturing. But the firm's communications planning approach—which emphasizes plans that cross the boundaries between traditional media, digital, and below-the-line vehicles—is gaining marketers' trust. When the agency expanded into the United States, it wasn't long before major advertisers such as Johnson & Johnson, Coca-Cola, and Nokia joined the client roster.

And there simply is no better measure of an agency's success.

THE AGENCY FUTURE

Without a doubt, the future will be challenging for ad agencies; for those that cannot or will not make the shift to Proposition 4.0, it may well be dismal. But, at the same time, there is a compelling reason to be optimistic: the reliance of marketers and media on advertising continues to grow. Here are three reasons why:

➤ First, the always-on world is one of rapidly expanding media options for consumers. And based on the digital experience to date, it is likely that advertising will continue to play a primary role as the economic mechanism to finance these new platforms.

➤ Second, in a world of expanding media and marketing complexity, marketers need objective and knowledgeable third parties as partners. Yes, marketers are doing more on their own, but complexity requires deep expertise, and it is too expensive and inefficient to insource the entire advertising and marketing services value chain, even for the largest and most sophisticated marketers.

➤ Finally, given the rise of private label competition and the brand proliferation that characterizes so many categories, agency partners who can help marketers deliver a differentiated message in the right place at the right time to the right consumer are more important than ever.

Of course, in order to meet the expanding needs and expectations of marketers, the agency of the future has to do a lot more than produce entertaining commercials. As the examples of WPP, Publicis, Crispin, and Naked illustrate, agencies must morph their service offerings, business models, and talent resources in multiple ways to catch up to the changing needs of their clients. This requires a richer package of services that address the creation, planning, and buying of advertising in traditional and digital media; it must also include the additional elements of consulting, product design, and technology. Further, it must master the data and analytics of advertising effectiveness and prove that its recommendations lead to results.

In short, the agency of the future must be more than an advertising partner—it must be a business builder.

Clearly this will require that agencies undertake ambitious change agendas. But there is no better alternative. Agencies must change their operating models to better meet marketers' needs, or die. And the sense of urgency is unlikely to dissipate. Take the example of London's Draft-FCB, which in October 2007 offered voluntary redundancy to *all* of its employees as a catalyst for completely restructuring its digital, creative, and production departments. Starting over like DraftFCB is clearly an extreme step. But advertising agencies do need to muster precisely this kind of courage to put everything on the table and secure a more prosperous future.

RESOURCES

➤ Berger, Warren, *Advertising Today*, Phaidon, 2004.

➤ Berger, Warren, and Crispin Porter + Bogusky, *Hoopla*, powerhouse Books, 2006.

➤ Goodrum, Charles A., and Helen Dalrymple, *Advertising in America: The First 200 Years*, Abrams, 1990.

➤ Hopkins, Claude, *My Life in Advertising and Scientific Advertising*, McGraw-Hill, 1966.

➤ Meyer, Martin, *Madison Avenue U.S.A.*, NTC Business Books, 1991.

➤ Morgan, Richard, *J. Walter Takeover: From Divine Right to Common Stock*, Irwin, 1990.

➤ Ogilvy, David, *Confessions of an Advertising Man*, Vintage, 1985.

➤ Ogilvy, David, *Ogilvy on Advertising*, Southbank, 2004.

➤ Rothenberg, Randall, *Where the Suckers Moon: The Life and Death of an Advertising Campaign*, Vintage, 1995.

➤ *The 100 Greatest Advertisements*, Dover, 1959.

➤ For more resources and up-to-date information, see www.businessfuture.com.

6

THE FUTURE
STARTS HERE

THIS BOOK IS TITLED *Always On* because there is no longer any downtime in advertising, media, or marketing. The pace is so relentless that the expression 24/7 does not do it justice. Think more in terms of 60/60/24/7. Every second, a connection is being made with a consumer somewhere. So marketers, media companies, and advertising agencies must be always on.

This new environment has had a powerful impact on consumers, too. "[Consumers] live in an always-on world. They are connected or know they always can be connected to media," says Beth Comstock, president, integrated media, NBC Universal. "They are engaged, in control, and eager to interact, not only with each other but also with their media—and to share that experience. [They] don't just talk at the water cooler. They e-mail clips, create mash-ups, and build buzz in ways that marketers dream about."

And, as the boundaries blur between advertising, information, and entertainment, consumers have become far more discerning about their media consumption. They know when marketers are trying to connect with them. And they decide whether advertising is worthy of their engagement.

In this new environment, marketers cannot win by wielding the implements of interruption that held sway over the captive consumers of yesteryear. Instead, they must create advertising that consumers will actually search out and find valuable—messages that improve life, make things easier, or entertain; messages that help consumers make decisions, connect with friends, and, most important, take action.

Creating advertising that powerful requires a carefully orchestrated mix of mathematics and creative craft. It is in some ways like playing baseball, where analytics (in the form of player knowledge and outcome probabilities) and broader insight into the game situation combine with personal brilliance (in the form of intuition and talent) to create base hits. And like winning baseball, successful marketing is all about increasing the percentage of hits and reducing the number of errors.

Now, as the future of advertising and marketing approaches, media platforms are abundant, advertising is ubiquitous, and technological innovation is constant. This has created a dynamic of discontinuity that can be navigated only with deep insights into consumer needs, interests, and behaviors.

For decades, these insights were limited by relatively basic analytics that could do little more than estimate the number of households tuned in to a TV program or the number of readers who flipped through a magazine. Today, with digital media feeding back insights to marketers as actively as they deliver information and entertainment to consumers, it is becoming possible to show an advertisement only to men who live in Los Angeles, who are between 18 and 34 years old, and who enjoy snowboarding and other kinds of outdoor activities. With this kind of knowledge, marketers (and their agencies) can move from a broader-based monologue to a more focused dialogue, tailoring their messages to specific consumers, precisely selecting those media that connect best with their target segments and more effectively influence their behavior. But this can be achieved only if the marketer is always on: paying attention, listening, and learning.

This shift to dialogue enhances not only the creation of marketing messages and the precise selection of the media platform best suited to delivering them but also the continuing refinement of the products and services being discussed. The two-way relationship with the consumer becomes part of a perpetual brand-building machine, and it ultimately can enable the marketer to move from insight to foresight.

Marketers, media companies, and advertising agencies are already in the process of adjusting to this more consumer-focused world. Many are developing new models that are aimed at creating relevance, accountability, and interactivity. Many are adjusting their media mix to focus on two-way platforms (see Exhibit 6-1). But as always, the mandate for change has been driven home more aggressively at some companies than at others. At some companies, the strategies and actions are even beginning to coalesce into road maps for success in this new

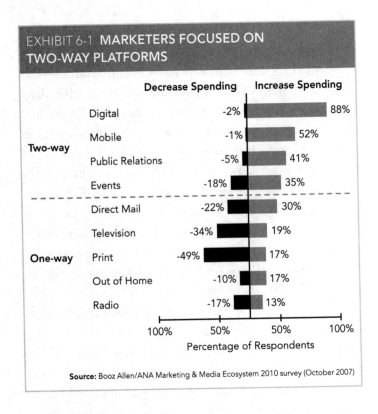

EXHIBIT 6-1 MARKETERS FOCUSED ON TWO-WAY PLATFORMS

		Decrease Spending	Increase Spending
Two-way	Digital	-2%	88%
	Mobile	-1%	52%
	Public Relations	-5%	41%
	Events	-18%	35%
One-way	Direct Mail	-22%	30%
	Television	-34%	19%
	Print	-49%	17%
	Out of Home	-10%	17%
	Radio	-17%	13%

100%   50%   50%   100%
Percentage of Respondents

Source: Booz Allen/ANA Marketing & Media Ecosystem 2010 survey (October 2007)

environment. These select few are already living in the future of advertising and marketing today.

MARKETER, HEAL THYSELF

At Johnson & Johnson, the eighth-largest U.S. advertiser, the future of advertising and marketing arrived in 2005, when the timing was right to break with the status quo and create a new model more in tune with an always-on world.

The catalyst at J&J was the departure of an esteemed senior marketing executive after 38 years of service. The company used the changing of the guard to recruit a new team of marketers drawn from media companies and advertising agencies, players purposely not grown from within or imported from other marketers.

The new team brought new skill sets and marketing mores to J&J. It shocked marketers across the country, as well as media companies and agencies, by pulling some $400 million out of the upfront buying season for broadcast TV. Henceforth, the act declared, J&J's business cycle and needs—not inventory availability on prime-time television shows—would drive the company's media-buying decisions. After all, the team reasoned, no one really knew 5 to 11 months in advance what J&J's marketing needs would be. So why commit to a broadcast schedule without sufficient confidence, based on consumer insight, that it was the right marketing solution to drive the business?

CONTENT DEPOSED

When J&J pulled out of the broadcast networks' upfront market, David Vinjamuri, adjunct professor of marketing at NYU and president of ThirdWay Brand Trainers, saw it as a sea change in the relationship between programming and advertising. He observed

> Johnson & Johnson's withdrawal . . . marks a decisive and permanent shift in the balance of power between content providers and advertisers that mirrors the power shift also taking place between consumers and advertisers, and is no less significant. Sumner Redstone famously said "content is king." There are still

> destination shows and superpower-scale events (like the Super Bowl), but there are now many, many options for content. Not only have the number and quality of television shows increased but they also now compete directly with Web surfing, satellite radio, podcasts, blogs, and other forms of new media for eyes and ears. Beyond that, the same content may be found in different distribution channels . . .
>
> What does this mean? It means that content providers must think carefully of consumer needs, distribution channels, and the revenue model for each and every piece of content they produce. It means that advertisers will increasingly be able to choose the platforms that they prefer to support and will get a say in how these function. And it mean[s] that consumers will ultimately accept or reject each model that advertisers and content providers present to them. Where consumers rejected individual shows before, they may now reject entire revenue models.

In the next year, the company decreased its overall TV presence, as well as its commitment to radio. J&J's expenditures in conventional media in the United States declined by more than $250 million in 2006, and its global investment in advertising was reduced by 10 percent to $1.9 billion. J&J's marketers also began insisting that its media buys include engagement guarantees. At the same time, the company increased the prominence of its direct-to-consumer programs, with a 31 percent increase in direct mail and e-mail efforts.

With new ways of quantifying advertising performance came new ways of planning it. Like many consumer goods companies, J&J's media planning had typically occurred at the end of the brand strategy process. Its primary goal had been aligning each brand's share of voice in the overall advertising spending in its category with J&J's growth objectives for the brand. Media choices had been based primarily on historic preferences and spending, virtually guaranteeing a heavy emphasis on traditional media such as television and print. As a result, there had been little emphasis on media and advertising innovation, especially among the company's largest and best established brands.

To counter this, the new team made communication planning the primary driver for media buying. Now, *how* the brands communicated to consumers, not *what* they communicated, became the key strategic focus. To reinforce the shift, J&J became one of the first major companies to create a communications planning review separate from the media buying and planning review process.

This decision ultimately led to a new association with the innovative agency Naked Communications, which was tasked with providing a more holistic and strategic approach to J&J's media planning and strategy. The move to bring in Naked was intended to be a catalyst for overhauling J&J's media mix in the always-on environment, focusing less on the day parts in the TV schedule and the circulation figures of print publications, and more on event programs, public relations, direct marketing, and digital media. Naked's mandate from J&J was simple, yet profound: direct our marketing spending to those channels that will create the most valuable connections between our brands and our consumers.

"We just weren't getting the kind of strategic thinking and return on investment for all the brands we represent," explained Kimberly Kadlec, J&J's chief media officer. "We were spending more on traditional media than we should have been, leaving some opportunities—such as search and experimental media—largely underleveraged. We were looking for innovative ways of approaching media—not just traditional media outlets but new, emerging media. Those opportunities need to be considered as part of the planning process to make sure we are investing wisely with an eye to the future."

The new marketing team revamped its talent management practices to accelerate the development of its internal digital advertising and marketing expertise. To address the digital skills gap, it initiated an innovative "externship" program that sent select J&J executives on three-month learning stints to its marketing partners, including AOL, NBC, Meredith Publishing, and BBDO. In turn, these partners were invited to send their executives to "extern" at J&J and obtain an intimate view of its brand priorities and decision-making processes.

All of these changes prepared J&J to expand its connection points with consumers beyond its areas of traditional strength, such as the retail point of sale and the doctor's office. Now, it began to address previously untapped digital touchpoints with consumers, seeking to ensure that J&J's brand and marketing messages were accessible online as well.

The development of BabyCenter.com is a good example of J&J's commitment to becoming more relevant and compelling digitally. When eToys declared bankruptcy in 2001, J&J rescued BabyCenter.com from the wreckage. At

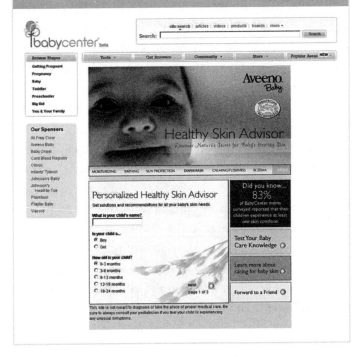

EXHIBIT 6-2 J&J'S BABYCENTER.COM ATTRACTS EXPECTANT PARENTS GLOBALLY

the time, BabyCenter.com was a content-focused, online destination for expectant mothers. Under new ownership, however, BabyCenter.com has been transformed into the largest online site in its category. Its audience is a high-engagement, loyal, and large social network of five to seven million moms and moms-to-be, who use the site for conversations, questions and searches, and transactions.

BabyCenter LLC (Exhibit 6-2) attracts more than six million visitors monthly to its sites in Australia, Austria, Canada, China, Germany, India, Sweden, Switzerland, the United Kingdom, and the United States. In the United States, it reaches over 78 percent of new and expectant moms online. In September 2007, it launched a U.S. site for Spanish-speaking consumers.

In building this online media platform, J&J created a relationship-marketing mechanism that directly and powerfully connects to one of its core consumer segments. BabyCenter.com is also an e-commerce site that creates leads for relevant merchants. All of this arises from the insight that moms want to share know-how and experiences with one another, as well as gain access to content and tools—personalization, comparison engines, shopping venues, and the like—that can make their lives fuller and easier.

While it still is too early to be certain that major marketers should "in-source" media ventures like BabyCenter.com, media ownership is a proven marketing model that harkens back to the early days of television. Efforts such as *General Electric Theater* and Procter & Gamble's soap operas drove some of television's initial innovation. Today, media vehicles such as BabyCenter.com, Nestlé's verybestbaby.com, and Kraft's kraftfood.com are enabling marketers to position their brands with the utility, relevance, and affinity that consumers seek. Product and

> "We've taken a media-neutral, consumer-centric, and brand-centric approach to brand objectives. Through integrated media planning, we're bringing very diverse talents and backgrounds together. What's critical is how we evaluate consumer behavior, how different forms of media connect, and how we can drive that to retail. If there's a way to engage and connect to our consumer in a more holistic way, that's what we're looking for."
>
> —Kimberly Kadlec,
> chief media officer, J&J.

brand messaging are indeed important elements of these digital destinations, but the key difference is that they are embedded in environments created to help consumers, not just interrupt them.

Media ownership is just one way J&J is engaging consumers in digital media. In 2006, the video series "Lonelygirl15" was a cult online hit whose origins were unknown. Today, Lonelygirl15 is a commercial venture, and J&J's Neutrogena skin care brand is one of its sponsors. In exchange, Neutrogena's Web site features Lonelygirl15 episodes—yet another connection to its target audience of females in their late teens and early twenties.

Of course, J&J's marketing transformation has not been without risks and costs. For instance, pulling out of the upfront in 2005 certainly gave the company greater flexibility to respond to brand needs as they arose. But that agility came at the expense of the pricing, scheduling, placement, and service benefits that historically have justified this annual buying frenzy.

But while itemized wins and losses may be hard to evaluate, the bottom line makes a powerful argument for J&J's new marketing approach. Despite its retreat from conventional media, company sales in 2006 rose by 6 percent to $53.2 billion. Perhaps more important, J&J is building today the capabilities necessary to be a marketing leader in the always-on future.

MEREDITH GETS THE BIG IDEA

In the always-on world, marketers are requiring more from their media partners. They want campaign development assistance and access to creative resources. They want proprietary research and consumer insight. They want the media platform integration that doesn't show up on rate cards. They want direct access to consumers. And they want the big idea. In short, they want many of the things from media companies that advertising agencies have typically provided—and more.

Sometimes the call for change is heard loudest in the least expected places, such as Meredith Corporation, a traditional media company with roots in magazine publishing and television station ownership, Based in Des Moines, Iowa, Meredith was founded in 1902 with the first issue of *Successful Farming* magazine, which is still published today. Today, the company is best known for its portfolio of largely women-focused magazines, such as *Better Homes and Gardens*, *Ladies' Home Journal*, *Family Circle*, and *Parents*. However, as its advertisers began to shift their marketing spending toward more custom media and below-the-line marketing, Meredith's executives recognized the need for a very different profile.

Thus, since 2005, Meredith has moved aggressively to transform the ways in which it creates value for marketers (see Exhibit 6-3). It started by leveraging its huge database of 85 million—primarily female—consumers and its custom publishing operation, which had long produced magazines for a diverse group of major marketers such as Carnival Cruise Lines, Chrysler, Kraft, and John Deere. Through these activities, Meredith had learned how to collect and manage information at an individual consumer level, mine the data for insight, and use it to develop both direct marketing efforts and more tailored media.

As part of a strategy to provide more agencylike services, Meredith has been systematically acquiring companies

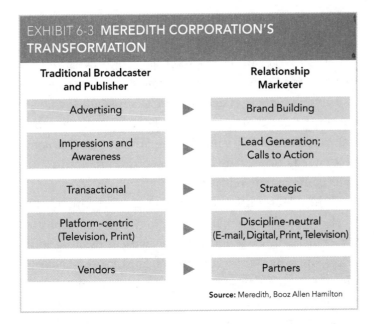

EXHIBIT 6-3 MEREDITH CORPORATION'S TRANSFORMATION

Traditional Broadcaster and Publisher		Relationship Marketer
Advertising	▶	Brand Building
Impressions and Awareness	▶	Lead Generation; Calls to Action
Transactional	▶	Strategic
Platform-centric (Television, Print)	▶	Discipline-neutral (E-mail, Digital, Print, Television)
Vendors	▶	Partners

Source: Meredith, Booz Allen Hamilton

that can help bolster its digital and customer-relationship marketing know-how. Since 2005, the company has purchased O'Grady Myers and Genex for their expertise in CRM and Web site development, New Media Strategies for word-of-mouth and Web 2.0 marketing, and Directive for database marketing and customer intelligence.

Meredith also made internal investments to form new groups to better respond to the changing needs of marketers. It founded Meredith 360 as a strategic marketing unit with both sales and creative resources, Meredith Experiential Marketing to fill the event-marketing space, and Meredith Video Solutions to provide video-content production and brand integration.

"Many clients prefer to have a single source for their marketing needs. Marketers want direct access to consumers and insight into their actual behaviors and interests," explained Meredith's Publishing Group president Jack Griffin. "More than just demographics, they want to connect with their target audiences in measurable environments that can drive a consumer response; they want to be able to use the media that make the most sense for the target consumers and their brands, whether it's print, video, online, or an event. And a media company, if it wants to compete, needs to provide all these services in addition to great content and great brands."

When Meredith put all of its new competencies to work, it was able to create more innovative opportunities for its marketing clients to connect with its existing audiences and other target consumers. For Clorox, for example, the media company launched an environmentally themed "Living Green" campaign that featured a home-show tour sponsored by *Better Homes and Gardens*, ad pages in *BH&G,* a custom site within bhg.com, and advertising on Meredith's TV stations. For Dodge, Meredith developed a targeted program for women that paired a half-hour *Family Circle* TV special with an online/print sweepstakes giveaway of a 2008 Dodge Caravan.

The ability to create broader, integrated, cross-platform programs such as these seems to be just what marketers wanted from Meredith. And better yet, as the always-on environment began affecting some of the company's business units negatively, others have more than made up for the shortfalls. For instance, in the first fiscal quarter of 2007, Meredith's television revenue fell by 7 percent compared to the same period the previous year, but the company's publishing ad revenue increased by 13 percent, and integrated marketing efforts grew by 50 percent—solid evidence that its realignment of resources was paying off.

THE NEXT GREAT
ADVERTISING AGENCY

Fortunately for agencies, many marketers will need guides to help navigate the increasingly complex media and advertising environment—trusted advisers who can help them make the right choices to connect their brands to consumers (and vice versa). If not for this need, agencies might become the "odd person out" in an always-on world. But to fulfill this role and once again become fully fledged marketing partners, agencies will need a fundamentally different set of skills from those they developed in the past.

The agency of the twenty-first century will establish its leadership through expertise in advertising innovation, analytics, and digital-technology know-how. And AKQA, a San Francisco–based advertising agency that specializes in digital-driven marketing, with offices in London, New

Marketers are putting digital at the core of their activity now. The problem they encounter is [what happens] when they work with the interactive department of an advertising agency and they don't get the thought leadership or ambition for the work. So there's a sense of frustration there, and that's why they are leaving the big bureaucratic traditional agencies, because you have to go through layers of people and process to get stuff done; instead, they're working with specialist partners who are becoming the client's lead agency, because—from a client perspective—they get a better layer of thinking, a more streamlined process and higher quality execution.

—AKQA chairman Ajaz Ahmed.

York, Washington, D.C., Amsterdam, and Shanghai, appears to have just the right skill set.

AKQA is a digital native, with a heritage in building business solutions (not just advertising platforms) in the online world. In fact, it has played a role in building digital infrastructure; AKQA collaborated with Microsoft to develop the user interface for Xbox 360, and it assisted with that product's marketing, as well. It is precisely this mix of capabilities in software development and interface design, paired with creative expertise, that gives AKQA an edge—for example, in linking insights about the use of digital products with the impact of digital advertising.

Just 13 years old, the agency operates free of the functional silos and layers of organization that have slowed the response of many older, larger agencies. It also has strong planning and analytics capabilities, which it applies to create holistic business solutions incorporating both analog and digital media. As AKQA'S CEO Tom Bedecarré says, "People live in a cross-platform kind of world; we approach engagements that way from the start."

AKQA also offers e-commerce and content management solutions. It has created Web sites, e-mail marketing, online advertising, and viral communications. Its media mix includes idea delivery on mobile phones, kiosks, digital organizers, DVDs, and interactive TV. And clients are beginning to ask AKQA to take on larger, more strategic business challenges, such as a request from Dell, Inc., for help in transforming its online strategy from direct response to brand building. "It's not just about building a big Web site," Bedecarré emphasizes. "It's about being able to demonstrate results."

A recent campaign for Visa reflects AKQA's ability to

deliver a results-focused, high-engagement solution: when Visa wanted to bring the "Life Takes Visa" brand campaign to digital media, the agency recommended a combination of rich media (generated by both professionals and users) and banner ads. It created a series of short Web videos to drive home the connection between Visa and the good life as illustrated by vignettes of real people actually enjoying and sharing their special moments. Real people also made their way into a series of banner ads that used actual photos consumers had posted on Yahoo!'s Flickr photo-sharing service. Finally, AKQA extended the campaign to mobile.

The digital rendition of the "Life Takes Visa" campaign delivered more than 594 million impressions within a single month. Further, engagement metrics revealed that visitors to the Visa site spent an average of five minutes there.

"What's impressive about AKQA is that they're always looking for something fresh and always working on new paradigms," said Jon Raj, Visa USA's vice president of advertising and emerging media. "It's not about creating banners and placing them on sites, it's about understanding what we need to accomplish. A lot of [agencies] talk about real life and then re-create the life they want to see. When you talk about life, you don't want Visa's interpretation; you want to see real life."

"We're not looking to go out and create a huge traditional offering, but our clients are asking for more integrated media ideas," adds Andrew O'Dell, AKQA's president of interactive marketing. "Our vision is to be known as an idea agency. It's not necessarily creative or media."

The blue-chip list of clients attracted to the idea of an

agency that can combine innovation, engagement, and results includes Target, Gucci, Dell, Nike, Microsoft X-Box, and Coca-Cola. It's no coincidence that this roster features a cross section of some of the world's major brands. The bigger the company, the more likely it is to have the resources to jump into new realms of advertising. "These very large agreements are important for us," says Tom Bedecarré, CEO, "but they also reflect what's going on with large marketers who want to see a bigger percentage of what they do shifted online." AKQA also appears capable of turning initial project work with these clients into much larger relationships. For example, AKQA is now developing the digital strategy globally for McDonald's and for Diageo's Smirnoff vodka.

For now, AKQA plans to remain independent and appears to have the capital to do so. In early 2007, General Atlantic, a private equity firm, bought a majority share in the agency for a reported $250 million. "We want to build the best digital network while at the same time keeping our independence and commitment to our founding values," explained Ajaz Ahmed. "During the process of the last few months, it was perfectly clear to us that our independence, the independent mindset of our company and our people, means a lot to our team and our clients."

Ongoing investments in technology will be an important part of AKQA's future. In August 2007, the company tapped into its cash trove and acquired SearchRev, a search marketing firm. Bedecarré explained the rationale for the purchase, saying, "We want to integrate a number of services for our clients so a CMO can optimize search against landing pages and so forth."

There are more deals to come—among the remaining

items on the agency's services shopping list are marketing optimization, mobile advertising, and other emerging media platforms. Similar to Google and Microsoft, AKQA aspires to automate media planning, search marketing, and marketing optimization. "It's about integrating the reporting of how dollars are spent and optimized across display, search, mobile, and all sorts of platforms. It's going to be technology run and optimized as opposed to media planners and analysts making decisions. I think a lot of it will be automated," says Bedecarré.

The best-in-class advertising agencies of the future may well follow AKQA's lead by melding brilliant creative—just like the old days—with technology, analytics, and consumer insight. Most of all, they will embrace their role as brand builders and business problem solvers. Finally, they will use their new tools and talents to help marketers create messaging and brand experiences that both capture consumers' attention and compel them to act.

MASTERING THE ALWAYS-ON WORLD

Periods of discontinuity are often painful, but they also represent major new opportunities for growth and market leadership. At no other time in the history of advertising and marketing has the potential been so great for smart players, no matter their size, to reinvent the game and win. For at no other time have marketers and media companies possessed so many compelling platforms to inform, entertain, and connect with consumers. And at no other time has marketing been so measurable, targeted, data-rich, and interactive.

But to bring in the new, marketers, media companies, and advertising agencies must first get rid of the old. Too many currently employed models of brand marketing, advertising agency management, and media advertising sales are obsolete.

These factors are sure to fuel a new era of creativity and innovation in marketing, advertising, and media. Already, the focus of advertising is shifting from talking at consumers to finding opportunities to be a part of their conversations and everyday lives. You may recall a prescient Fabergé Organics shampoo commercial from the 1970s, which implored consumers to "tell two friends." In this famous spot, images of the Fabergé model replicated across the screen as she told two friends about the product, and they each told two friends, and so on until the screen was full of Fabergé devotees. It is this kind of social referral, endorsement, and advocacy that advertising needs to aspire to today. And the good news for marketers, agencies, and media companies: the tools, methods, and media channels to accomplish this are available as never before.

New tools and media channels require new ways of working and organizing. As the current models of brand marketing, advertising agency management, and media advertising sales become obsolete, new skills and processes will be applied to integrate ideas and campaigns. The "integrators"—the marketing and advertising professionals of the future—will excel at turning the cacophony of choice across suppliers, media channels, and ideas into a symphony of brand integration and business results.

Whenever value chains are reconfigured (and that's exactly what's happening now), it almost always creates a new set of winners and losers. The winners, among marketers, media companies, and agencies, will be those that learn to reconfigure their businesses in several important ways. They will:

➤ Develop brand-messaging and entertainment experiences that consumers actually want to seek out *and* share—offerings that engage consumers and turn them into advocates and influencers.

➤ Use the skills of relationship marketing and insight development to listen, learn, and engage directly with consumers; to focus on their interests and behaviors, not just their demographics; and to know them better than anyone else.

➤ Build campaigns that seamlessly bring together above-the-line advertising and below-the-line marketing to achieve greater sales impact and more measurable results.

➤ Develop new technologies, applications, and consumer environments that accelerate marketing and media innovation.

➤ Learn how to measure the real impact of different media on campaign performance. And use those results to understand how well each medium best drives the marketer's perennial objectives of brand awareness, trial, purchase, and loyalty.

➤ Put organizational systems, compensation structures, and metrics in place to encourage—not constrain—advertising and media innovation.

➤ Redesign sales, planning, and creative processes to put

the consumer's needs at the center of marketing as well as media.

Pursue these objectives successfully and you can be assured of a vital role in the always-on future of advertising and marketing.

RESOURCES

➤ Schley, Bill, and Carl Nichols, Jr., *Why Johnny Can't Brand: Rediscovering the Lost Art of the Big Idea*, Portfolio, 2005.

➤ Schultz, Don E., Stanley I. Tannenbaum, and Robert F. Lauterborn, *Integrated Marketing Communications: Putting It Together and Making It Work*, McGraw-Hill, 1993.

➤ Springer, Paul, *Ads to Icons: How Advertising Succeeds in a Multimedia Age*, Kogan Page, 2007.

➤ Stroud, Dick, *The 50-Plus Market: Why the Future Is Age Neutral When It Comes to Marketing and Branding Strategies*, Kogan Page, 2006.

➤ Vinjamuri, David, *Accidental Branding: How Ordinary People Build Extraordinary Brands*, Wiley, 2008.

➤ Zaltman, Gerald, *How Customers Think: Essential Insights into the Mind of the Market*, Harvard Business School Press, 2003.

➤ For more resources and up-to-date information, see www.businessfuture.com.

NOTES

Chapter 1

2   "Gone are the days of 'one shoe, one advertising campaign.'": "On Madison Avenue, A Digital Wake-Up Call," *Wall Street Journal,* March 26, 2007.

2   "As *Advertising Age* reported, 'Neither Nike nor Wieden officials would get into specifics . . .'": "Wieden & Kennedy Will Not Take Part in Nike Review," *Advertising Age,* March 2007.

2   "We get right to the center of the consumer . . .": Ibid.

3   "The company has invested about $2.5 billion in endorsement contracts extending through . . .": Nike Inc., 10-Q Filing, April 4, 2007.

4   "From 2003 to 2006, Nike grew its U.S. revenues from some $4.6 billion to nearly . . .": Nike, Annual Reports and 10-K Filings (various).

4   "In fact, the percentage of Nike's budget devoted to traditional media . . .": *Advertising Age,* 100 Leading National Advertisers, 2005 and 2007.

4   "It's really all about going deeper to get deeper connections and deeper . . .": "When Great Ads Aren't Enough," *ADWEEK,* March 19, 2007.

7–8   "For all the hype around digital advertising and media, for instance, the top 100 national advertisers . . .": *Advertising Age,* 100 Leading National Advertisers, 2007.

8   "Consumers' viewing and reading habits are so scattershot now that many advertisers say . . .": "Anywhere the Eye Can See, It's Likely to See an Ad," *New York Times,* January 15, 2007.

11   "Does advertising increase demand for a given firm's products . . .": Neil Borden, *The Economic Effects of Advertising,* Irwin, Chicago, 1942.

11   "If 90 percent [of the audience] do not remember it . . .": Randall Rothenberg, *Where the Suckers Moon,* Vintage, New York, 1995.

12   "The spurious distinction between image advertising and retail advertising . . .": Randall Rothenberg, "Bye-Bye," *Wired,* January 1998.

16   "We know there's a shortage of interactive . . .": "Coke's Got Many Digital Pushes, but One Goal," *Advertising Age,* August 27, 2007.

18 "We keep planning on the basis of . . .": Richard Rawlinson, "Beyond Brand Management," *strategy + business*, summer 2006.

21 "It is no wonder two-thirds of our senior marketers believe their . . .": Ongoing research, Booz Allen/Association of National Advertisers.

Chapter 2

40 "We've never been able to get to this level of granularity . . .": "How Marketers Hone Their Aim Online," *Wall Street Journal*, July 19, 2007.

41 "Students don't see credit-card issuers or financial institutions in general . . .": "A For-Credit Course," *New York Times*, September 30, 2007.

41 "This puts [that Facebook group] in the upper ranks of the . . .": Ibid.

49 "These efforts have been promising enough for CEO A. G. Lafley to proclaim, . . .": "P&G Will Boost Marketing Spending for Fiscal '08," *Advertising Age*, May 2, 2007.

54 "Everybody is talking about communities now, and so the question is . . .": "Smaller, Private Communities Get Significantly Higher Levels of Customer Engagement, Says New Communispace Research," Communispace, Inc., company press release, March 20, 2007.

54 "Founded in 1999, Communispace has created more than 250 custom online . . .": "Community Participation Trends and Drivers," Communispace, Inc., http://www.communispace.com/3_news/perspectives.asp.

63–64 "For example, according to research from the National School Boards Association . . .": National School Boards Association (NSBA) and Grunwald Associates LLC, *Creating and Connecting: Research and Guidelines on Online Social and Educational Networking*," August 2007.

67 "Talking to them about things other than the product . . .": Booz Allen Hamilton, "Marketing and Media Ecosystem 2007," presentation to the annual meeting of the Association of National Advertisers.

68 "Eventually, AB hoped to build up the Bud.tv audience . . .": "Brew Tube," *New York Times Magazine*, February 4, 2007.

68 "Yet, despite an initial investment of somewhere between $20 . . .": "Bud.TV on Tap for Another Year," *Hollywood Reporter*, September 26, 2007.

70 "We're also trying to find ways to create a dialogue . . .": Ibid.

70 "In 2008, the company plans to spend some 10 to . . .": Ibid.

72 "According to the marketing research company BIGresearch . . .": BIGresearch, "Simultaneous Media Survey (SIMM VIII)," August 10, 2006.

72 "Moreover, searches for 'Pontiac Solstice . . .': "The Apprentice Is No Novice at Driving Sponsor's Web Site Traffic," Hitwise.com, April 25, 2005.

72 "Not only did Pontiac sell 1,000 of the special version . . .": "Pontiac Scores with TV-Web Promo on *The Apprentice*," *Direct*, April 19, 2005.

75 "And it predicts that by 2010 . . .": "Virtual Worlds Are Trendy Spot for Kids and Teens," *eMarketer*, September 2007.

Chapter 3

82–83 "By 2004, the number was only four. . . .": "Marketing Trends," presentation, Diageo Investor Conference, April 26, 2007.

83 "Some of these ad networks have corralled . . .": comScore, Ad Focus rankings, August 2007.

84 "Almost 70 percent of consumer purchase decisions are made at the shelf . . .": "Shopper Marketing: Capturing a Shopper's Mind, Heart and Wallet," Deloitte/Grocery Manufacturers Association, 2007.

84–85 "According to a study by the Grocery Manufacturers Association and Deloitte and Touche, . . .": Ibid.

94 "In 2007, Ed Erhardt, president of ESPN customer marketing and sales, indicated . . .": "Media Guide: 360 Mix," *Advertising Age*, November 6, 2006.

97 "According to MTVN, its Virtual Laguna Beach draws users to the site . . .": "MTV Goes 4D with Virtual Worlds Push," *CNET News*, March 29, 2007.

97 "And although Second Life gets great press . . .": "Virtual Worlds Platforms and User Numbers," *Virtual World News*, October 1, 2007.

97 "According to MTVN's metrics, 99 percent of the consumers . . .": "MTV Goes 4D with Virtual Worlds Push," CNET News, March 29, 2007.

99 "We believe there is power in aggregating that content, and we believe in ubiquitous . . .": "The Hubub over Hulu," BusinessWeek.com, August 2007.

Chapter 4

109 "But lately marketers have become less interested in . . .": David Verklin and Bernice Kanner, *Watch This, Listen Up, Click Here,* Wiley, 2007.

117 "Exposure has very, very weak correlation with purchase intent and actual sales, whereas an engagement . . .": "Engaging at Any Speed? Commercials Put to Test," *New York Times*, July 3, 2007.

121 "With its reports, IAG was able to show that Sepracor's sleep aid Lunesta was both the most recalled prescription . . .": "Lunesta Continues to Top the Charts as the Most Recalled Prescription Drug Advertising, but Watch Out: Here Comes the Competition," IAG research, June 5, 2007.

126 "Resigned to the reality of widespread adoption of C3 . . .": *MediaPost Publications*, November 5, 2007.

129 "Case in point: Nielsen's ranking for the 2007 season . . .": "Nielsen: Grey's Most Played-Back Premiere," *Mediaweek*, October 15, 2007.

131 "By May 2007, that number had doubled to 10 million.": "Data Reveals Online Having Profound Shifts on TV Viewing, Navigation Too," *MediaPost Publications*, September 27, 2007.

131 "If you look at the future of audience measurements, where you are measuring exposure across . . .": "Start-Up Rivals Target Nielsen," *Variety*, February 17, 2007.

132   "Advertisers are demanding and asking their agencies to provide solutions that match up with how their brand . . .": "ESPN, Nielsen Take Step Toward 'Total Audience' Measurement . . ." *Advertising Age,* October 17, 2007.

132   "Nobody likes a company that has too much power . . .": "Start-Up Rivals Target Nielsen," Variety.com, February 17, 2007.

136   "To that end, in the fall of 2007, the company announced that it planned to develop . . .": "Google Prepping Big Brand Marketing Dashboard," *MediaPost Publications,* October 25, 2007.

Chapter 5

142   "More than half of these same marketers also said they expected to make further revisions to their agency roster within the next year. . . .": "2007 Marketing Outlook," CMO Council.

145   "In the 1960s if you visited . . .": "The Challenges Facing Today's Business Leaders," *Journal of Direct, Data and Digital Marketing Practice,* May 15, 2007.

150   "As Shelly Lazarus, Ogilvy & Mather's chairperson and CEO says . . .": "Shelly Lazarus Wants Media Back at the Table," *Advertising Age,* November 19, 2006.

152   "You have a coordination problem when you have two people in an organization . . .": "The Challenges Facing Today's Business Leaders," loc. cit.

154   "A study by Evalueserve for Sapient, a global interactive agency . . .": "Electronic Media, Marketing and Advertising Buyer Value Study," Sapient and Evalueserve, December 2006.

160   "Our long-term fantasy is we walk up to you and you give us say, $10 million . . .": "Google Tests New Ad Offerings? But Will Advertisers Follow?" *Wall Street Journal,* December 14, 2006.

160   "Microsoft wants to be a leader in advertising as well . . .": "Microsoft to Increase Ad Business," *New York Times,* October 2, 2007.

162   "And, with $22 billion in cash on its balance sheet . . . , it seems likely that Microsoft . . .": Microsoft Corporation, first quarter 10-Q filing, September 30, 2007.

163   "Gillette then returned to Openad.net for ideas on how to translate Live 1's . . .": "Gillette Taps 9,000 Creatives Online," *Advertising Age,* September 17, 2007.

165   "In 2006, these services contributed 53 percent of WPP's revenue . . .": "Acquisition of 24/7 Real Media 2007," WPP company presentation, May 2007.

167   "Says Sorrell, 'WPP is the only company in our industry to do . . .": "The Challenges Facing Today's Business," loc. cit.

167 "What we see is a massive, massive transfer of investment...": "Publicis Plans to Buy Digitas to Add to Online Presence," *New York Times,* December 21, 2006.

169 "We will partner with them as we partner with CBS, ABC, Time Warner...": "It's an Ad, Ad, Ad, Ad World," *New York Times,* August 6, 2007.

172 "It spoke directly to the 16 million consumers who visited Boots locations every...": "Is Mad. Ave. Ready to Go Naked?" *Fast Company,* October 2005,

174 "Take the example of London's DraftFCB...": "Mass Redundancies Offered at DraftFCB," BrandRepublic, October 11, 2007.

Chapter 6

181 "Johnson & Johnson's withdrawal...": "The Upfront Vanishes," ThirdWayBlog.com, May 15, 2006.

182 "J&J's expenditures in conventional media in the United States declined by more than...": "Johnson & Johnson Pioneers New Marketing Rules," *Advertising Age,* May 23, 2006.

182 "At the same time, the company increased the prominence of its direct-to-consumer...": "Johnson & Johnson Reallocates Budgeting in Favor of Online Marketing," *BizReport,* March 20, 2007.

184 "Those opportunities need to be considered as part...": "The Envelope, Please," *JNJ BTW,* July 17, 2007.

186 "We've taken a media-neutral, consumer-centric...": "The Reinventor, Kim Kadlec," *Media Industry Newsletter,* November 1, 2006.

187 "Despite its retreat from conventional media, company sales...": *Advertising Age,* op cit.

190 "And a media company, if it wants to compete, needs to provide...": "Meredith Expands Marketing Services Portfolio, Acquires Directive," *Media Daily News,* MediaPost Publications, October 5, 2007.

190 "For Dodge, Meredith developed a targeted program for women that...": "Meredith Serves Up 'Holiday Party,'" *Mediaweek,* October 30, 2007.

190 "For instance, in the first fiscal quarter of 2007, Meredith's...": "Q1 2007 Earnings Call Transcription," Meredith Corporation, October 24, 2007.

191 "Marketers are putting digital at the core...": "Q&A: AKQA's Ajaz Ahmed on Internet marketing," e-consultancy.com, February 6, 2007.

192 "As AKQA'S CEO Tom Bedecarré says, 'People live in a...'": Ibid.

192 "It's about being able to demonstrate results.": "AKQA Poised for Expansion,..." *San Francisco Business Times,* August 3, 2007.

193 "When you talk about life, you don't want Visa's interpretation...": Ibid.

194 "During the process of the last few months, it was perfectly clear . . .":
"Q&A: AKQA's Ajaz Ahmed on Internet Marketing," econsultancy.com,
February 6, 2007.

194 "We want to integrate a number of services for . . .": "AKQA Buys
SearchRev; More Deals to Come," *Online Media Daily,* August 23, 2007.

195 "'I think a lot of it will be automated,' says . . .": "AKQA Adds Search Tech
Firm," *Adweek,* August 22, 2007.

INDEX

ABOUT THE AUTHORS

CHRISTOPHER VOLLMER (vollmer_christopher @bah.com) is a Vice President in Booz Allen Hamilton's Global Consumer and Media Practice, based in New York, and he leads the firm's North American Media and Entertainment team. He focuses on growth and portfolio strategy as well as advertising and consumer marketing in the media, entertainment, and consumer products industries.

Since joining the firm in 1995, Christopher has worked with the senior management of many of the leading global media, entertainment, and consumer goods companies. He has helped develop innovative growth strategies, strengthen operating performance, and redesign organization structures. His clients span a wide range of businesses, including television, music, film, magazines, video games, sports, broadband/digital, wireless, and consumer goods.

Most recently, Christopher has led the firm's Future of Advertising campaign, which has focused on how marketing and media are being redefined by digital technologies and new business models. His work in this area resulted in the article, "The Future of Advertising Is Now," which appeared in the Summer 2006 issue of *strategy+business* and provided the initial inspiration for *Always On*. His subsequent interviews with leading marketing and media executives later appeared in *CMO Thought Leaders: The Rise of the Strategic Marketer* (strategy+business books, 2007).

Christopher holds an MBA from the Wharton School of Business at the University of Pennsylvania and an MA in International Studies from the University of Pennsylvania. He also graduated with a BA in English from the University of California at Berkeley. He lives in Old Greenwich, Connecticut, with his wife and two children.

GEOFFREY PRECOURT (gprecourt@mac.com) is a writer and editor who lives in western Massachusetts. He has served as an editor-at-large for *strategy+business*, contributing editor of *Fortune*, and deputy editor of *Smart Money*, and was the founding editor of *Adweek* and *Agency* magazines. He is the editor of *CMO Thought Leaders: The Rise of the Strategic Marketer* (strategy+business books, 2007).

ACKNOWLEDGMENTS

The "future of business" series has been a collaborative effort from the beginning. Herb Schaffner, the publisher for business books at McGraw-Hill, spotted the potential in a book about the future of advertising and marketing and helped initiate this series. We also wish to thank our collaborators at McGraw-Hill, who walked the extra mile to produce this book and bring it to market, including Ruth Mannino, Eileen Lamadore, Seth Morris, and Ed Chupak.

This book was developed and edited under the auspices of *strategy+business*, the quarterly magazine published by our firm. We would like to thank the entire *s+b* team for their roles in a project that required its own innovative approaches to advertising, marketing, and media. In particular, publisher Jonathan Gage played an extremely significant part in conception, marketing, and strategy; managing editor Elizabeth Johnson and project manager Gretchen Hall took on much of the difficult and essential work of coordinating images and permissions; literary agent Jim Levine made a great contribution; and publicist Mark Fortier and marketing manager Alan Shapiro helped bring the book to the attention of the world at large. Ted Kinni, senior editor for *s+b* books, played a major role in developing the book's quality and clarity. Art Kleiner, editor-in-chief of *strategy+business*, was directly involved in this project from its beginnings as a magazine article; his steady stewardship and resolve kept the entire *Always On* team on track.

Lisa Mitchell, the director of the firm's Marketing & Sales Service Offering, played a vital role in coordinating every aspect of this project. She served as the central point of communication and capably unraveled the knots that threaten every book's progress. Every author should have such a partner.

This book would not have been possible without the contributions of the many outstanding individuals who make up the talented team at Booz Allen Hamilton and are focused every day on delivering results for the world's leading companies. *Always On* indeed benefited tremendously from a platform of support, collaboration, and insight that is rare in any enterprise. Adam Bird and Les Moeller, the two partners who lead the firm's Consumer and Media Practice globally and in North America, respectively, were enthusiastic about this project from the start, which had its origins in our original Future of Advertising work, and provided a steady stream of encouragement and ideas. Vice Presidents Gregor Harter, Edward Landry, and Andrew Tipping developed the book *CMO Thought Leaders*, which provided some of the conceptual foundation and research on which this book was based.

Further thanks also go to the extended team, which includes Harry Hawkes, Jeffrey Tucker, Matthew Egol, Richard Rawlinson, Patrick Behar, Scott Corwin, Paul Leinwand, Steffen Lauster, J Neely, Rich Kauffeld, Patrick Houston, Cesare Mainardi, DeAnne Aguirre, Gregor Vogelsang, Alexander Kandybin, Jack McGrath, Tim Blansett, Jose

Baquero, Carlos Navarro, Tom Casey, Thomas Kuenstner, Laurent Colombani, John Jullens, Steve Treppo, Karla Martin, Thomas Ripsam, Martha Turner, Yogesh Pandit, Michael Fischer, Maria Boccella, Bart Sayer, Karen Premo, Leea Nash, Elizabeth Hartley, Nick Pachetti, Nami Soejima, Carolyn Ude, Nikhil Bhandare, Wendy Millan, Michael O'Rorke, Daniel Silberman, Vessela Genova, Leslie Hampel, Serafima Iofina, Medea Nocentini, and Josephine Prechter.

Booz Allen alumnus Randall Rothenberg, now the CEO of the Interactive Advertising Bureau, deserves recognition for his contributions, including coauthorship of the article, "The Future of Advertising is Now" (s+b, Summer 2006), which helped lay the foundation for *Always On*. We are also grateful to the organizations whose collaborations helped inform this volume: the IAB, the Association of National Advertisers, and the American Association of Advertising Agencies.

Jill Vollmer, Christopher's spouse, deserves special recognition for providing the family support required to complete this book, which consumed many nights and weekends, and as important, for her invaluable insights as a marketer. Her objective, real-world perspective helped make *Always On* a much better book.

Finally, a debt of gratitude is owed to the many clients in media, marketing, and other sectors whose experiences and, most important, successes informed the insights and perspective that now is *Always On*.

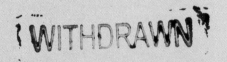